Sparks From
The Fire of Time

Sparks From
The Fire of Time

Rick & Louisa Clerici

NEW FALCON PUBLICATIONS
TEMPE, ARIZONA, U.S.A.

International Standard Book Number: 1-56184-130-7
Library of Congress Catalog Card Number: 97-65817

First Edition 1998

Cover art by Denise Cuttitta

The paper used in this publication meets the minimum requirements of the American National Standard for Permanence of Paper for Printed Library Materials Z39.48-1984

Address all inquiries to:
NEW FALCON PUBLICATIONS
1739 East Broadway Road Suite 1-277
Tempe, AZ 85282 U.S.A.
(or)
320 East Charleston Blvd. • Suite 204-286
Las Vegas, NV 89104 U.S.A.
website: http://www.newfalcon.com
email: info@newfalcon.com

DEDICATION

To Josephine Gray, whose faith and light helped bring life to this book.

ACKNOWLEDGMENTS

As I sit at my computer, cup of java in hand, it is a beautiful, golden, autumn afternoon in New England. A warm,
soft breeze floats in through my window and my thoughts
turn to the warmth of friends and loved ones, all those
who gave their love and support to Rick and I during the
process of birthing this book.

To our students in the "Clearing the Connection"
series, Rick and I have learned much from you. To everyone at the First Spiritualist Church in Quincy, MA, especially Rev. Larry Hilton and Phyllis Hilton, thank you for
your support. Also to friends, Beth Delong, Dick
McArthur, Jan Brink, Gita Beth Bryant and Robin Carroll.

Most of all, to our family, Rob and Cam Clerici, Harold
and Josephine Gray, Pat and Paul (Polar Bear) Davidson
and Lee Dalghren, there are no words complete enough to
express to you and the rest of our family, our appreciation
for all you have done for us. To my brother Larry Gray and
my wonderful sister Kathleen, and Jessica and Jonathan
Gray; you have all inspired us, have made this book
possible.

To my mother, Joey, there is no way full enough to
thank you, and Pat Davidson who truly is the Godmother
of this book, who typed and gave us her strength from the
beginning... Wow! Without you both, this book would not
have been published.

To Ruth Montgomery, thank you for loving this book.
To Dr. James Wanless, thank you for your timeless
Voyager. To Marilyn Gordon, Bennett Litwin, James
Twyman, Henry Leo Bolduc and Jamii Szmadzinski...
wonderful words. And last, but certainly not least,
Nicholas Tharcher, our Editor and wise one. Rick and I
thank you all, soul-deep, may your fire sparkle and speak
with us on the path.

Louisa Clerici

TABLE OF CONTENTS
(Titles in Italics are Stories)

INTRODUCTION

This book you are about to read, my book, our book, is a story of a magical adventure that spans a period of two earth years. I should say, perhaps, that this is just one leg of the journey because the journey continues even now. As you open this book, I feel as though you are signing on for this splendid expedition, joining us in our quest.

You will be our companions as we sail the silver strands into other worlds, and explore the crystalline tunnels that spiral through time. And like us you may be changed by the journey. Be ready to open your eyes and mind and heart, perhaps forever.

Now that I've seen the explorer in you, let me tell you, as far as I possibly can, who we are.

I am Louisa Clerici, a woman, a teacher and a therapist living in the present. I have been a psychic and medium since I was a small child. Ever since I can remember I have been able to sense events before they occur. As a young girl, I came to realize that I was able to communicate with beings or spirits that most other people were unable to see or hear. And as I grew up in the U.S.A., immersed in the popular culture, I was somehow able to keep intact that delicate connection with spirit. Over the years, I have studied with many talented and caring teachers and worked to develop my talents and abilities. I have participated in and witnessed an amazing array of psychic and spiritual phenomena including spiritual healing, channeling, prophesy and materializations (the visible appearance of spirit energy). Yet the events and occurrences of these past two years have startled me and filled me with awe.

The stories in this book were presented to me, in a manner that I will later describe. Each and every word came through me unchanged. The process is one that I find intense and most often breathtaking. To this day, I am amazed that such wonderful stories can be told through me, a person who normally finds it difficult to write a letter to a friend.

The framework of this book, the personal account of these past two years, even this introduction, have been written by my husband, Rick Clerici. Based on volumes of my notes and thousands of conversations, he has taken on the task of putting into words my deepest feelings, sensations and intent; being my voice in this book.

Rick works as a therapist and musician/songwriter. Over the past twenty-five years, he has studied extensively in the areas of psychology, healing, and metaphysics. Rick has been my closest companion for nearly fifteen years and I suspect, in many other lifetimes. As the events in this book unfolded, Rick was always emotionally and spiritually supportive, always there with me searching for deeper levels of understanding. Rick, having shared in these experiences so intimately, is the perfect person to put this incredible saga into words.

The stories themselves, these elegant tales from other worlds and times, were given or transmitted to me by people from the future, and the *writers group*. It is with great intensity and emotion that these future people send us their stories, and it is the love and skill of the *writers group* that give the stories form. The *writers group* is best described as a group of beings who exist in the spirit or non-physical realm. Much of what we know of them is surmised, as they prefer not to be the topic of discussion and would rather have the stories be the focus of attention. A few of them have been well known writers in other times and yet, they are happy to remain anonymous and write in this collaborative effort. The *guides*, to whom I often refer, also exist in the spirit or non-physical realm and are beings who give me personal guidance in my life. I have been aware of my guides since I was a child.

The stories are truly the jewels that you will find along the path of our journey. They are tales about our world, our planet, other worlds and other times. Some of them are like windows that look into times yet to come, and some of the stories are like mirrors that reflect back to you your most intimate thoughts and struggles.

The theme that runs through all the stories is the theme of transformation. The stories reveal the subtle nature of the transformative process. In the midst of our pain, grief, fear and most ordinary moments, the opportunity to transform is always present. Transformation brings understanding and meaning to all the trials and mysteries of our lives; it embraces all the moments and fragments and seeming coincidences and weaves them into a seamless fabric of complete change.

Where the stories address the future, I believe they do that in the same time honored manner of all prophesy. I feel, as do many other students of metaphysics, that prophesy is not an attempt to describe what will be, but rather what very well might be. The future, it seems, is not etched in stone but is constantly being chosen and created. Many metaphysicians and physicists feel that there are future probable worlds that are pre-physical, real in some level of existence that is not yet physical. These worlds are projections of the directions that we are traveling in now, and as we approach them closely enough to bring them into physical reality, we do so by choice. Of course we move in these directions by collective and individual choices, and it is possible to alter outcomes, no matter how probable they might seem. One of the elements in the creating of reality, one of our guiding lights, is the information available to us through prophesy. Prophets and artists have, throughout time, warned us of certain paths of action and encouraged us along other paths.

If you are disturbed or frightened by the worlds you encounter in a few of these stories, remember that they are intended as warnings, warnings that are gifts to us as we make choices and decisions, and literally create our future.

These stories of transformation are like shooting stars that, in those fleeting moments of their passing through our world, capture our imagination and move us to dream and create. Let these *Sparks From The Fire of Time* lift and illuminate you.

1

THE ADVENTURE BEGINS

Beginnings are so elusive when you really look for them. As I look back now, searching for that point in time where the events in this book began, I realize that a subtle process of preparation had long been under way. It is as if my whole life was quietly growing towards these events. And yet, there is a day when this lifetime of training blossomed dramatically. I mark this day as the beginning.

My dreams have always been very vivid and alive. I have clearly had many precognitive dreams and I have always been aware of the tremendous power and mystery available in the dream state. But none of my dream adventures could prepare me for the incredible course my dreams were to take. I'm still not quite sure that the dream that began this odyssey was really a dream at all.

A friend had just been rushed to the hospital for what seemed to be a serious infection. The doctors, uncertain of the reason for this infection, had begun treating him with intravenous doses of antibiotics. My friend was of course scared and as I spoke with him over the phone, I tried to hide my concern and help him calm down to begin the healing process.

Immediately after our conversation, I sat down to meditate and send absent healing to my ailing friend. I quieted my thoughts, and began to visualize my friend, Paul, when something very peculiar happened. I started to drift, almost too quickly, into a very deep meditation. In a moment, I seemed to awaken somewhere in what appeared to be a dimly lit tunnel. It was very strange to feel wide awake and yet to find myself not in my room but in this odd tunnel.

I could feel myself drifting and swaying as I tried to orient myself. I attempted to move, to walk, but walking felt suddenly alien. It was a struggle for me to move just a few feet forward. As my eyes adjusted, I noticed that there were lights at both ends of the tunnel and appearing at irregular intervals on the ceilings, walls and floor, were holes of varying sizes. Somehow I sensed that these holes were doors of some sort and in that same moment, I simply climbed through one of the openings into a beautiful, lush world. I was completely startled to be standing on the ground, sunshine and trees everywhere, with a clear blue sky, expansive overhead.

I turned to survey the scene and saw, right beside me, a Native American man sitting calmly on his horse. Without his speaking, I felt his thoughts form in my mind. In a few short moments, a telepathic conversation took place. I told him that I was concerned about my friend's health and that I was trying to send him absent healing. The man on horseback assured me that Paul was receiving healing energy and then he said something that made no sense to me. He told me that *now* I would be able to return to the tunnel any time I wanted to. I couldn't imagine why I would want to return and the incongruity of his statement and the dream-like surroundings left me bewildered. Yet I felt a sense of inner knowing when he told me that there were many people and places awaiting me.

When I awoke, I realized that this meditation was deeper than any I had had in a very long time. This meditation turned "dream" was an entirely new experience for me. The following night I would have a dream that would convince me that enormous changes were taking place, changes that, in some yet unknown way, would put to the test my most solidly held beliefs.

The next night I experienced a series of, what I now call, tunnel dreams. In the dream, I found myself walking or trying to walk in that same dimly lit tunnel. I felt nearly overwhelmed by a sensation that was something like trying to walk through an invisible field of energy or into a very strong wind. This feeling was heightened by the near absence of gravity. My steps felt bouncy and uneven. My body grew somewhat accustomed to this new environment and as my walking became less tentative and more steady, my awareness of the surroundings became sharper.

The lights at both ends of the tunnel appeared as tiny luminous specks. I guessed that the tunnel must be very long. In the distance, I could see a few other people just pop into the tunnel, and then flounder around trying to get a footing. I felt both filled with apprehension and bristling with energy as I walked into the tunnel's depths. There was a sense of stark clarity as in a lucid dream and a feeling of unconscious moving and seeking as if somewhere inside, I knew where I was going and what I was looking for. I was filled with a kind of awe as my emotions wandered from fear to wonder to an odd feeling of detachment. A silky electricity hung like a moving mist in the air and currents of feelings and information flowed around and through me.

Finally, for no real conscious reason, I was drawn to enter one of the mysterious holes. It was there that I met Frederick and it was there that my odyssey of wonderful dreams and stories began. Over the course of the following year, my life ebbed and flowed through these stories of light and moments of wonder, as I tuned my inner ear to these beings, who lovingly passed tales and verse through holes in the wall of time.

2

Meeting Frederick

Saturday, June 13th, was a day sweet with the ordinary moments of life. My husband, Rick, and I took a long brisk walk in the morning. As we always did on our walks, we talked endlessly about our dreams and plans. We discussed my tunnel dreams and Paul's illness and, of course, speculated about the man on horseback in my first dream.

I was tempted to allow the tunnel dream to become just one of those beautiful, breathless moments that blossom so profusely in spring. A psychic and medium since childhood, I had become, to some extent, accustomed or adjusted to extraordinary experiences, though adjusting is a constant ongoing process. Rick was always open and enthusiastic about my abilities and experiences, and ever ready to offer his own insights and comments. I was able to explore and discuss my feelings concerning these dreams, and maybe it was this comfortable flow of discussion and thinking that allowed me to simply move on to other thoughts. There were, at this time, so many other things to think about.

June was filled to the brim with projects. Rick and I had just finished moving into a larger apartment, and most of our belongings were piled in the corners. We were also in the midst of preparations to open our own private practice in hypnotherapy. Tables were covered with lists, books, papers and memos. My mind sometimes felt just as cluttered. There was a restless moving in my soul, and each second seemed to flicker with illumination and newness. That night, as I held Rick close to me, I was so innocent and unaware of how deeply my life would be altered by those next few hours of sleep.

Sometime during those next few hours I had three tunnel dreams. In the first dream, I found myself in that same tunnel struggling to walk through the thick, vibrant atmosphere. I felt sharply aware of being physically there and, at the same time, I sensed a deep knowing of purpose moving far below the surface of my awareness. The first dream ended almost as quickly as it started.

In the second dream, my maneuvering skills improved. I saw other people in the distance trying to walk. Their motions looked awkward, almost futile, as I'm sure mine had, only moments before.

In the third dream, I walked for some time past many holes, until I was drawn very forcefully towards and into a hole that opened into another world. I looked with wonder at a beautiful, tropical garden. A solitary man sat waiting on a stone bench. "My name is Frederick, I have a story to tell you," he said.

I sat down quietly on a bench that felt strangely familiar. And I listened with all my heart. His story and life opened to me like a dark, red rose, filling all my senses, and even appearing like a living play in my mind's eye. I could literally see and feel everything that he described. I was deeply moved, overwhelmed, lifted on the wings of his words.

Still reeling with the story's urgency, I found myself unexpectedly floating back through the hole. Almost instantly I woke up, feeling totally out of place in my bedroom, feeling as though I had been dropped from another world. My mind was swirling with questions and confusion, while fragments of scenes and emotions floated in my memory.

I climbed out of bed, grabbed a pencil and paper, and began scribbling down notes as fast as I could. I only seemed to remember bits and pieces and yet, I clearly recalled his very last words, "You will come back."

I wasn't sure I could go back. I didn't really know where back was. Questions came in waves, one upon the other. Should I try to go back to sleep, or perhaps meditate. Or would I simply find myself there again? When I sat back in my mind, I felt stunned and unsettled, and yet the better part of me was very curious.

In the days and nights that followed, I began to find it increasingly difficult to concentrate on every day concerns. Behind every thought, every tree, was a feeling that drew me back into that tunnel and into the garden. I wondered if I would ever see Frederick again or hear his wonderful story. I wondered, too, just what it all meant. I tried to decipher the tunnel as though it were a secret code or message.

I think, even then, that I was developing a subconscious sense of my place in all this. Somehow I knew, without words or signs, that I was to become a messenger between worlds. A few days later, on June 19th, I had another tunnel dream that revealed to me even more of this role that, already, I was beginning to accept.

Once again, in the midst of a normal sleep, I found myself in the tunnel walking. This time there was an even richer quality to the experience. I seemed to have a deeper awareness of myself and my surroundings. I felt more agile, more powerful and decidedly more conscious. Much to my surprise, I began to feel like an explorer, curious and excited. Before too long I came to a hole, and without hesitation, I climbed in.

I climbed right into the same lush garden. And as I stood there drinking in the warm perfumes and chorus of bird songs, I suddenly realized that I was very glad to return and that at some level, I knew the way back. I wasn't even surprised to see Frederick, sitting on the stone bench, waiting for me. He seemed pleased to see me and anxious to continue his tale.

Frederick was a very special man who radiated warmth and compassion. There was an urgency of mission that animated his every action. Frederick's words took flight, twisting and turning, soaring deep into my mind. Sometimes I was stung sharply by those words, so filled with emotion, and often I became tangled in the delicate web of ideas and events. As I sat mesmerized on that cool stone bench, Frederick's tale, vivid scenes, smells and sounds were etched in my deeper memory. Then, almost as suddenly as he had begun, Frederick drew his unfinished story to a close. He simply said, "You will hear more later. I will be with you when you write. You must write this story down, remember it."

Once again I awoke, feeling a little at sea in my own room. Wide awake at five a.m., and filled with a tremendous energy, I was compelled to leave the room, shutting the door quietly behind me, and write down everything I could remember. I sat at the kitchen table, in the soft morning light, and began writing, with incredible intensity, the thoughts that came into my head. The flow of words came faster, and the scenes and descriptions seemed to pour from every part of me.

Almost between one breath and the next, I switched from remembering and reporting, to taking dictation while listening to Frederick's warm, persistent voice. For over forty-five minutes I wrote feverishly. Frederick spoke quickly, sensing the delicate line between us, and I managed to get every word though my hand began to cramp with exhaustion near the end. The end came suddenly and graciously, even silently, and though I was breathless with excitement, I had just enough energy to find my way back to bed, and drop instantly off to sleep.

I woke up bright and early, only a few hours after my writing frenzy, and excitedly told my husband Rick, every detail of my strange experience. I was filled with energy and questions, and we both tried to understand or make some sense of these events. Rick and I talked about dreams, lucid dreams and astral travel, and we speculated endlessly. As we examined each detail again and again, I began to feel that even my expanded definition of dreaming lacked the impact that I was looking for. This was far more than dreaming or being lucidly in control of a dream. *I felt that I had actually traveled to some real world to meet Frederick.* But what place or world that was, and how I had come to be there, I really had no clue.

Later that afternoon, I decided to try to write down more of what I remembered. I had the urge to use the typewriter this time, so I sat down in front of it not know-ing what to expect. Almost immediately, words began flowing into my mind as I typed quickly and steadily. I was surging with energy and inspiration, and only stopped once, when I saw Frederick's face clearly in front of me. I knew that Frederick was there to bring his story to me. He tried his best to convey to me how important his story was to him and how much he wanted it to be recorded and passed on. He also said he wanted it to be called *The Gardens of Rio.*

I typed without planning, direction or even thinking. There was a knowing that guided me to the end. When the end came, I sat in silence, stunned, waiting. The story was finished, that I knew, and yet I had to read it to see that it was real.

The story read beautifully, it flowed so gently, and it was filled with the life and feelings of this deeply compas-sionate man. I felt I could see into the man through his story, into his heart and soul. I could feel his dilemma, the pain of his inner turmoil and his overwhelming need to speak, to warn us, to help us. I don't know exactly why, but I sat, then, in front of my typewriter, and cried. I guess I cried in sheer release of energy and tension. And yet much of my crying was for the beauty of Frederick's story, his caring and love for this world, and for the precious act of creation that we had just shared.

Frederick's story signaled an incredible change in my life. My psychic and dream experiences exploded with intensity. The dreams and stories that began to flow into my mind shook me to the core. These new ideas forced me to expand my view of reality and question many of my beliefs. I felt as though I was being flooded with light, shaken from my ordinary trance, and allowed to catch a glimpse of the hidden worlds that surround us all.

I give you the experience of reading this first story with just a few last thoughts. I believe that Frederick is a real person, who lives somewhere in time, even now as you read these words. I believe that his story is true, and that the lessons he has learned he wishes to pass on to you. You may find, as I did, that much of this information is difficult to accept. I suggest that, just for a few moments, you suspend some of your beliefs, become like a child and surrender to your innocence. Listen with your heart and soul and perhaps you will hear some of the love and wisdom dancing in the lines of this story. Open your heart, and if you dare to let go, you may feel the wondrous vibrations sent to you from Frederick Generald, a man who lives, now, somewhere in the tunnels of time.

3

FROM THE TIME TUNNEL:

THE GARDENS OF RIO

The year was 2041, and everything was going so well, when I don't think I had a complaint in the world. Yes, the life of Frederick Generald was content and full. I spent June in this very villa in Rio, and I actually had three whole days of peace here, three whole days when the world seemed to stop. There was not one call from the office of Generald Co., business was going incredibly well, the children did not call. Even Marcie, my dear wife, was in a good mood for those three days, no, I must be dreaming. But then again, I would have to look back on that time as the beginning. But the beginning of what, I don't know.

The villa we owned in Rio was my favorite place in the world. Of the four homes we owned, I really only enjoyed myself in Rio. The villa was called, La Sol Fuerte. It was so quiet and so peacefully hot. There were always fewer interruptions here, and less pain. For once Marcie had readily agreed to come this June. She was recovering from mouth surgery and didn't feel that she looked good enough for our more social life in Paris. She looked good enough, she always looked good enough. She could easily pass for twenty-nine, even though she would be forty in September. All twelve of her operations had cost a lot, for me. Not in money, there was always plenty of that around. The real cost was the pain that always was between us. I always thought that she looked great, but Marcie would never be happy. She would never again be the nineteen-year-old artist's model I met in Dallas so long ago; but then I didn't want her to be. Her mouth always looked fine, but her words never would. Most days were one fight after another. But today MM was happy, planning her next social season of events.

Everything was good, too, at Generald Co. headquarters. Sales had topped 1.2 billion last year, and Tonki (as I call him) my only friend and Vice President of Generald, felt they would double this year. I hate to admit it, but sometimes I don't care. My father and uncle would roll over in their graves. Generald had been their lives, *but it wasn't mine.* Generald was the largest tobacco company in the world, but for me it was only numbers on paper, Tonki on my back, travel and pressure. But on a more positive note, escape from Marcie.

Actually, when I look back, life was simpler then. Business was good. Generald was one of only two tobacco companies in the world, and actually all the business was ours. Things in the world were quiet and had settled down since the great storm, and Marcie was busy.

The last night we spent in Rio, then, I had a dream. I never, ever dreamt, at least I had not for ten years or more, probably the medication, so the very event of dreaming was strange.

The dream itself shook me so hard, I woke up feeling like someone was strangling me. I dreamt I was out in my garden, sitting on my bench, and a very tall, black figure approached all at once. The sight was so horrible, there aren't words to describe it. The figure seemed to be dressed totally in black, with the traditional gloves, but the gloves had claws, pointing at me, coming for me. Grotesque, huge and black, the figure wore a large mask-like helmet that gave me a feeling of horror like I have never known before. A deep, unreal sounding voice said only, "Who are you?" And then I was awake and filled with a deep terror. The mask stuck in my mind for hours and days.

Back in Paris, life seemed to resume as usual. There were decisions that had to be made, and Tonki had so many solutions and ideas, as usual. But I was more tired than usual. Something had changed, but nothing had changed. Had I changed? I didn't think I did that. Marcie said that change was only for people whose lives were not as perfect as ours. Perfect, I didn't feel perfect. Marcie always said feelings were unnecessary for people whose lives were perfect.

This perfect little life of ours went on as usual until the tenth of July, when it happened again. I awoke screaming at three a.m., screaming and crying, a grown man of forty-two years old, begging the Gods to let him live. The head, the mask, etched in my mind, for what would turn out to be forever.

The black mask, so grotesquely big and ugly, it seemed like this must be a visitor from some hellish planet, always in black, every inch covered. Was there a human body enclosed in that hellish space suit? That seemed to be a question I woke up with. And the feeling that this devil wanted me, in some way, for some deed, was waiting for me. Where? Why me?

Try as I had to, I could not get the picture of the black figure out of my mind. It seemed to be a part of my every day life now. I tried to chalk it up to stress, life in a strange world, and Marcie, especially Marcie. My best friend in the world, David Sleigh, Tonki to me ever since our childhood friendship began, said the dream symbolized my unreleased frustrations with life. Marcie said it was starting to make her nervous. MM and David were the only two people I ever told. One very hot August night, after I had had the nightmare a total of four times, I was now afraid to go to sleep, and for some reason afraid to wake up. MM and Tonki demanded I see a doctor. The doctor demanded I relax. It was time for a vacation.

In September we went back to Rio, and I began to sleep again. Tonki said it was Rio. Marcie said it was the medication. I didn't care.

I began to feel more at peace in Rio, more accepting of the fate that awaited me. And that was the feeling that I had, that some fate out there was waiting for me and at some moment, would surely appear again. I don't know why, but I had given up, I was ready.

MM thought she would use the time in Rio to have her eyes lifted again, she said to match her new, more upturned mouth. It was a very simple procedure, as all cosmetic surgery was, standard. Standard Marcie as usual.

She was back at the Villa within hours, bandaged only for two days. We tried to avoid each other as much as possible. But on one particularly electric, Rio morning, outside enjoying the garden, I was startled by screams piercingly loud. There was no mistaking MM's high pitched screech. When I arrived in her bedroom, I found her out cold, lying on the floor, bandages beside her, surrounded by surprised servants. She came to, as the doctors arrived and she seemed to be in shock. She was raving that the doctor had turned her face black and disfigured. She had to be forced to look at a mirror and see her, as usual, beautiful but very pale face.

I don't think I had ever seen Marcie stunned until that day. The doctor's calming shot soon put her to sleep. The doctor asked why Marcie was so nervous. Under a strain?

Back in my garden, I knew MM was never nervous. What had she seen when she stood in front of her beautiful mirror and pulled her bandages off as she had done many times before? Who had she seen?

MM blamed me of course, all my ludicrous talk about nightmares was making her edgy. She was soon her usual self again, and she wanted to go back to Paris. I knew I couldn't leave, not yet.

The night before MM's trip back to her home territory, I found I couldn't sleep. I felt uneasy. The night seemed to hang in the room, flaunting itself. At three a.m. I got up, thinking I might get a breath of fresh air in the garden, when MM burst into my room, hysterical, her face a deep red-black, screaming my masked man had been in her room. Never in my life had I ever seen anyone so terrified. She said it was my fault. I don't think she had ever before experienced a moment that real.

The next morning, she went back to a small clinic just outside of Paris. It took her a long time to recover. She refused to see me and we didn't see each other again for five years.

I stayed in Rio, unable to leave, numbed by the last few months, months that seemed like years. By October my days consisted of sitting in my garden, eating very little and staring at the walls all night. I didn't want help. I think I knew it was coming.

And it did come, on October 30th, in the moments before dawn. I left my hot, airless, sleepless bedroom, and crept outside for air, my stone bench seemed unusually cold, in contrast to the hot, steamy, pre-dawn mist, and I waited. I didn't have to wait too long. My nightmare seemed to form very, very slowly, in a flash in front of me.

I felt paralyzed but strangely unafraid, more shocked that my moment had come, at last.

"Don't be afraid, tell me who you are," a deep muffled voice said through the mist.

And I did.

"My name is Freddie Generald, and I own Generald Co., the largest tobacco company in the world." The words flowed, as if pouring from some tremendous fountain. Every moment of my life seemed to take shape, coming straight out from my soul. And I felt strangely at peace, showing my life to the tall black mask in the mist.

As streaks of light came through the hot mist, the words stopped. My stranger sat down next to me, and as the sun came up in Rio, the figure, with both black, hideous, hand-like gloves, lifted the mask-helmet up high and off. This revealed the most shocking and unexpected sight I've ever witnessed in my life! It was a woman!

She had the reddest, gold hair I'd ever seen, it seemed to blend with the sun rising in the sky. She was tall, and had the only warm eyes I've ever seen.

Her voice, unmuffled by the thick mask, was easy and light. "My name is Alara; I'm sorry I frightened you. I come from the earth year 3017. This is only the protective clothing we wear every day. Without it, we can't breathe our air and live. Some of us are very adept at traveling, and I was chosen because I'm especially experienced. The air of Planet Earth has deteriorated so badly, I've been sent on this journey into the past, to "see" and to try to bring back understanding to the people of 3017. We know the problem started with many civilizations, during many different times. We want to understand what happened to our Earth. I want to show you something ..." She handed me a picture of my garden, taken in June of 3017.

We had a lot to talk about. Alara and I sat on that stone bench until moonlight streamed across my precious garden.

Then she took my hand and said, "Thank you Freddie. I have many more places to go on this journey, but some day I'll come back and we'll talk again. Same place, different time."

As the black mask faded into the moonlight, my life stopped, and began again.

The next morning I left for the Generald headquarters in Paris. It would soon be a very different kind of company.

There was much work to do, and I've spent the rest of my life doing it. The few times when my hope dimmed, when the work seemed to be too much for me and the opposition seemed too strong, I had only to look at that picture of my garden, taken in June of 3017, and my energy was renewed. That picture was the greatest gift anyone ever gave me.

I am only one man, and there have been many men working against me and with me. I've worked hard for my cause, all the gardens of Rio and the Planet Earth.

The rest of my life has been very busy, very purposeful, and I'd like to think, may have changed the year 3017 a little.

Five years after my fate met me, I went to see Marcie.

And a very long·time later, Alara came to visit me again, in that garden in Rio, just as she said she would.

We talked for a long time, as the moonlight streaked and danced everywhere. And she promised to write my story.

4

BEAUTIFUL NEW WORLDS

The Gardens of Rio is a story that blooms with healing and awakening, and yet, for me, there were also some very disturbing, even alarming ideas. The very first line, beginning with, "The year was 2041," sent a chill through my body. How could a man be telling me what had happened to him, in the year 2041? Frederick was describing a series of events that took place in his past, and yet his past was still in my future. The more I pondered this bizarre twisting of time and sequence, the more confused I became.

Something about Frederick's strength and sincerity compelled me to open my understanding to deeper possibilities. There was a part of me, even then, that knew he was telling the truth, but my rational mind kept fighting tooth and nail.

In some respects, the last line of the story was an even greater threat to my sense of reality. The words, "and she promised to write my story," hit me like a bolt from heaven. The implications of that line were staggering, and at first I rebelled furiously. *I* was the woman that promised to write Frederick's story. *I* was the woman that sat on that stone bench listening, and then later writing feverishly. *I* held that story in my very hands, *me*, Louisa Clerici, in the present, not someone called Alara, from some far away 3017. As I struggled with these contradictions, odd feelings welled up in me, and my mind raced from one possibility to another. Frederick spoke to me in that moment, and his words cut a clear path through the tangle of thoughts when, in referring to Alara and me, he said, "They are one and the same."

For a moment, my world stood breathlessly still. In that place inside, where I perceive, process and understand, everything was silent, as though some secret had escaped, and every creature and fragment of my reality feared for it's life.

Something slowly began to change in me. My reality of the present began to wear thin, began to seem transparent. Ordinary reality took on a dream-like quality, seemed less solid. Even the ground that I walked on felt odd somehow. At times, the scenes of everyday life appeared to be only a version of reality, based on my beliefs. As my beliefs shifted, I began to feel as though I was walking through many different realities or versions of reality, at once.

Up until this time, I had believed in theories such as reincarnation, in a more intellectual way. Even my model of reincarnation was limited and simplistic. I believed, more or less, in a straight line of lives leading from the past towards the future. I believed that each life is built on the last life, taking the accumulated wisdom to move on and expand the experience of living. Well, my experience of living was expanding so quickly that I felt dizzy!

I had read about world views that described time as an illusion, that all time exists now, future, past and present all existing somewhere in various levels or expressions of reality. I loved to read Carlos Castaneda's brilliant descriptions of non-ordinary reality. I thought that I understood that one's perception of reality is based on beliefs and descriptions. But as the beliefs and descriptions shifted radically, my hold on reality became tenuous. The experience of time travel was much more unsettling than I would ever have imagined.

Rick and I took long walks and talked nonstop about the ideas in Frederick's story. We theorized, guessed, speculated and imagined until our minds ached and our senses cried out. I prayed for guidance and searched the corners of my soul for answers. I knew I had to let go of my limiting belief system, but these new beliefs were so vast, perhaps limitless. Rick struggled with his own beliefs and shared his questions and discoveries with me. My spirit guides, beings who have communicated with me since childhood, reassured me and urged me to continue on. And my higher self, that eternal, wiser part of me, helped to prepare me for this broader, richer experience of life.

A wordless knowing began to bloom inside me, a knowing that transcended beliefs and feelings. The inner battle began to subside, and in its place grew a clarity of purpose. I knew, at least on one level, that I did indeed walk in many different worlds. I was Louisa Clerici, a psychic and medium living in the 1990's, and for some yet unknown reason, I had the ability to step through holes in time and visit people and places in both the past and the future. I also knew that in visiting these other places and times, I would meet the *me* that had gone on to be born again and live in future times, such as 3017.

Through the dreams and experiences that I've had, I have, over time, come to terms with this natural progression of *me*. It feels right to me now, the idea that the Louisa that lives in the 1990's and travels to distant times in her dream states, might be born again, perhaps many times, and live in the year 3017, where she is still traveling, with perhaps more clarity and purpose. I can see this now, in the moments of my deepest meditations. I can feel how it will all take place, a natural progression of talents, abilities, directions and desires.

This first story is perhaps the dearest to me because it opened up so much for me, and in me. The story showed me that love can reach beyond the most incredible boundaries. The love that Frederick feels for life and the planet, compels him to reach out, even beyond time.

Like many of us, Frederick let a great part of his life slide by, living in the shadows of other's expectations and accomplishments. Happiness seemed to elude him. But then no one around him was happy and he began to feel that, perhaps, that was just the *way* of life. Though he was very frightened, he had the courage to see the truth, when confronted with it. And in seeing the truth, he was transformed.

Frederick passes on to us this light of transformation. It is both our burden and our opportunity.

The strong sun of Frederick's garden reached out through time and touched me. It was with a new sense of vitality and inner peace that I began traveling to other times, returning with dreams, stories and messages of love.

5

THE MESSAGE

A whirlwind of activity seemed to sweep through the six weeks following my journey to *The Gardens of Rio*. I dreamed, wrote, meditated and tried, as best I could, to catch my breath and keep my balance. In my dreams, I visited beautiful new worlds, and encountered intriguing people and spirits, all anxious to tell their stories through me. I often sprang from the bed, in the middle of the night, to sit at my typewriter for hours, remembering, listening and typing. At other times, I would awaken with fragments of countless stories floating in my mind, all waiting for the opportune time to unfold, alive and whole. The fragments of stories seemed to be reservations for some future time, when the remainder of the story would be sent for completion.

I got the feeling at this time, that there was perhaps an infinite treasure of stories waiting to be told through me. And the stories were so powerful, compelling and maybe limitless, that I guess I feared losing myself in this process. I began to feel the need to know how much, if any, control I would have as this journey unfolded.

My growing desire to share these beautiful tales slowly began to outweigh my apprehension and confusion. I think, even then, that I knew that this material was being sent through me for many eyes to see and hearts to feel. Though I could barely imagine what writing a book would entail, I clearly had a sense that it would be my task, if I chose to go on.

I could feel my life changing; it felt like butterflies in my soul. As the changes progressed, the color began to fade from some of my usual interests. I could feel myself moving into new patterns. In my newly forming life, even amidst the uncertainty, a sharpness and clarity began to appear.

Both Rick and I felt this contrast between confusion and disorder, and inner knowing. Our lives were being, not so quietly, disrupted and yet, it felt strangely good and right. A balance was forming between my insecurity and resistance, and a deep inner direction and acceptance.

One morning, after dropping Rick off at work, I began to feel a, now familiar, strong bodily vibration. The feeling settled in, intense and unchanging. I wasn't sure if the feeling signaled the presence of one of my spirit guides or a story about to come through. The sensations are very similar. But on this particular morning I just wasn't in the mood for guides or stories. I scolded whoever it was, saying, "Leave me alone, I can't deal with this now; I have a lot to do in the real world. I've already said I couldn't receive another story for at least a week." (I was trying to exert some control in this process.) I immediately felt someone say, "Relax, we're not here to disturb you. We are here in response to your call. You have been calling us and we are here only to help you."

I instantly felt calm, and realized that what they were saying was true. During our morning drive and walk, Rick and I had discussed the stories and what they meant to us. As usual, there were a great many questions that I wanted answers to and, as I sometimes do, I appealed to my guides for answers. Remembering my questions and confusions of the morning helped me to relax and realize that my guides had come to help, not to intrude. It's really very easy to forget the things that we ask or wish for and, later, find ourselves surprised when we get what we wanted.

Finally relaxed and comfortable, I sat at my kitchen table, coffee and pen in hand, and tried to reestablish contact with my guides. I sat quietly sipping my coffee and drifted deeper and deeper into a trance. After what seemed like a short time, I heard a strong male voice say, "What are your concerns?" "I'm not sure," I said, "Sometimes I feel a little confused about everything that's happening. And I can't quite believe that I could channel material that is good enough to be published. Is it really possible or true?" The voice responded, "Everything is as possible or true as you believe it to be. You have the choice of negating any experience that you have. Why are you so concerned with what is good enough? Ask yourself why you are so concerned with being good enough, with your work being good enough. Think on these things."

The response took me a little by surprise, but I continued on. "I'm also afraid that I won't be able to control these experiences. I'm concerned that the stories will get in the way of my every day responsibilities." The voice answered me, even more firmly. "I say that you are in complete control. You have total control of every part of your life, as does everyone. But my words are not enough for you. You must go deep within yourself and you will realize this control. To realize this now would be of great value to you personally, no matter what path you take in your life."

I don't think I've ever received a completely straight answer from one of my guides. Their answers always make me feel deeper for clarity, force me to go back into myself for the answers. In my stronger moments, I'm thankful that their guidance is gentle and subtle. In my weaker times, I'd like all the answers spelled out in black and white. Their guidance once again caused me to dig deeper into my attitudes and beliefs, and in doing that, reaffirm my faith in myself and my abilities.

I came to think, at that time, that I had already chosen to write the stories and eventually a book. I felt that the decision was made, that I had thought everything over and, though still somewhat tentative, I was ready to go on with the project. I didn't understand that my usual and vague kind of decision making process was not what the universe had in mind. I would soon find myself plunged into a fire that would test my faith and forge my strength, in preparation for a final and unequivocal decision.

6

THE EAGLE SPEAKS

The last Friday in July was a sultry summer day. I took the train to Boston and barely made my business appointment. The city was a flurry of sound and movement. The air over automobiles rose in shimmering waves of heat.

As I left my appointment, my mind was on slowing down and cooling off. I bought a large iced coffee to go, found my way to a nearby waterfront park and sat down in the shade on a park bench. The cold coffee was like nectar and the shade and the ocean breezes created an oasis on the edge of the sweltering city madness. I felt such relief sitting there, lost in a dreamy moment of ordinary thoughts and concerns, when I suddenly felt someone's presence nearby.

I looked around quickly, but there wasn't anyone even remotely near. I felt a delicate tingle on the back of my neck that made me suspect a different kind of presence. I quieted myself, closed my eyes and prepared to view that inner landscape. Immediately I was staggered by an incredible vision, a vision of an immense bird standing right in front of me. My senses reeled at the sight of a bird, much larger than myself, a luminous white eagle with deep piercing eyes. There was something very majestic about the way he stood, as the breeze rustled the edges of his snow white feathers. The eagle, with an air of purpose, lifted his expansive wings to expose a large sparkling purple stone. For some odd reason, his action seemed to make me feel very safe and protected. I was astounded at how peaceful and serene I began to feel.

Without a sound or words, he spoke. "You have a choice to make." "Yes I know that," I said, and in that moment I really did know that. "Do you think you have the courage to face the fear?" he asked. "Yes," I replied, and somehow I felt that I had. The eagle fixed me in his gaze. "Their stories will be etched on your heart so you will feel them. It will not be an easy job to write them but you will have help. There will be seven days in which to choose."

I opened my eyes and I could still see him looking at me, his eyes glistening in the sunlight. I closed my eyes and, although the vision was fading somewhat, I knew that he could still hear me. "I know that I have the strength and courage to complete this task. I feel as though I've been preparing for this work for a very long time." I really felt ready and strong and yet, I knew that I was to take the full seven days to make this final decision.

The eagle faded slowly from sight and my mind raced to fill the vacuum that he left with a million thoughts and images. One of my thoughts was a reminder to meet my mother for lunch. And so, dazed by the morning's events, I tentatively made my way to the subway for what I thought would be an uneventful ride and afternoon.

The subway station hummed with activity, the stream of people on escalators slowly converging on an ocean of faces that bobbed up and down on the platform. There was a dream-like quality to the motion and sound, and the heat seemed to make colors run and my clothes stick to my skin. I surrendered to the stream of movement, floating with the crowd into the train, pressed together, as each moment swelled with odd expectancy.

The air in the train was thick and filled with the smells of sweat and perfume. The doors clattered shut, the lights flashed, people reached for plastic seats and chrome poles as the car lurched to a start and rolled forward into the dark tunnel. A man leaned forward and asked me for the time. As I looked at his face, I was seized by the impression that he was a swirling body of energy. His clothes, his eyes, his arms, all energy whirling and pulsing in different colors and patterns. I mumbled the time, without thinking, and then looked past him only to find the train filled with other beings of light and energy. Even the air was visibly textured with movement.

An older woman pulled at my sleeve and put her lips near my ear. "What time did you say it was?" Her hoarse whisper sounded like wind through dry leaves. The train rocked and bumped as it picked up speed. I showed her my wrist, hoping she would see my watch, but she asked again and I was forced to answer her. My mind raced, and the train rocked on faster and faster. Just then, I saw a minister, white collar and black shirt, standing only a few feet away. I wondered why I hadn't noticed him before. He had such an odd look, such a different vibration. As I watched him, I was overcome by the feeling that he was going to die soon. A pale, lifeless light surrounded his face, and as the train bounced on even faster, I wondered if this would be his last ride, this day his last day.

Suddenly I was filled with fear. I knew the train was out of control, headed for a crash in which we would all die. I couldn't believe that I hadn't seen it coming. I couldn't believe that I was going to die in this way.

As quickly as my fear had filled me, I found a strange, deep sense of peace and power growing and then towering above the fear. I felt, somehow, as though I could keep the train from crashing. The fear raged, energy flashed in the car, and yet I wanted to stay on until the last stop. The power and fear were both equally present. I found myself calmly accepting that it was equally possible that I might live or die in the next few moments. I was surprised when we rolled to a stop at the station and very, very relieved.

As I walked away from the train, I looked up at the station clock, amused to see how little time had passed. I walked on to meet my mother and pondered the lesson or test that I had just experienced or survived.

I could feel that this test had been about time and fear. I wasn't sure if I had passed the test or completely understood the lesson. I couldn't help but wonder what other trials might be in store for me.

7

In A Hail Of Bullets

I awoke, Saturday morning, to the sound of crows in the distance and the smell of summer that drifted in through the bedroom window. I sifted through the soft remnants of dreams, thinking that I would discover the Eagle and the train ride there, but instead I found that they were very *real*. As I mused on those memories, picturing the strange events of yesterday, I could feel the silent presence of the Eagle, watching me, protecting me. Eyes closed, I looked for him, looked for that vision in my mind, and saw nothing. And yet I knew that I was caught in his piercing unseen gaze, held in the quiet wonder of his thoughts.

My husband, Rick, woke up and we laid there talking about eagles, decisions and how our lives were changing. Rick tried to remain objective, saying that he would support me in my decision, whatever it was. Yet he voiced the opinion that so much of my life seemed in preparation for this task. I had the feeling that somewhere the Eagle nodded his approval.

I felt strong and practically convinced that I had already made my decision. So it surprised me when I began to swing back and forth between decision and indecision. As the day progressed, I found myself firm and decisive one moment, frightened and full of doubt the next. The arguments for either choice became equally compelling.

In the following days, very little changed. I seemed to swing from elation to deep concern and then back again. I listed, in my mind, the pros and cons, the positive feelings and the fears. I could feel the Eagle's calm, persistent presence, always just out of sight, in some corner of my awareness. I knew that he listened to my questions and pleas but he said nothing, gave no answers, only watched without judgment.

Near the end of the week, the sky began to clear and most of my feelings started to fall into place. On the one hand, it was very possible that this was a once in a lifetime opportunity. On the other hand, it was also possible that this commitment might entail years or the rest of my life. I knew, also, that writing the stories would propel me into strange and sometimes frightening worlds and would push me beyond the safety of my beliefs and opinions, changing *me* in the process.

It's funny, I really seldom feel that I'm a brave person, often quite the opposite. But it was the challenge of change and growth that finally tipped the scales in favor of writing.

In the end, after a long sorting-out process, the decision still felt awesome and final.

It was on the first of August that I made a pact with the Eagle and perhaps the universe. I agreed to write down these stories, as they came, without answers or explanations. I knew I had the strength to experience the unknown and the desire to bring these tales to my world and time.

My decision to go on with the writing brought me a feeling of complete freedom. Ever since the first story, I had been oscillating between commitment and fear. Deciding meant taking responsibility and letting go of that feeling of being stuck. I was pleasantly surprised at how making a commitment seemed to break a dam and allow me to flow into new, exciting discoveries.

One of my discoveries was that it was time to begin teaching a psychic and spiritual development class that I had long wanted to start. Over a period of fifteen years, I had been fortunate enough to have studied with some very gifted spiritual teachers. I applied myself diligently, studying forms of meditation, methods and levels of trance induction, and many avenues of spiritual seeking and expression. From the best teachers, I learned that real spiritual discovery involves following that quiet, simple path that leads even deeper inside one's self to the *higher self.*

I had long suspected that, often what passes for spiritual teachings, is really only the offering of security, rigid answers and paternalistic comforting. I was beginning to feel that many people were ready to seek knowledge in a free and open environment, without the rigid dogmas and mandatory belief systems. I wanted to create a class in which students could explore their own potentials, expand the horizons of their awareness, test their own beliefs, and perhaps touch the nature of their personal purpose and mission.

As I looked inside myself, I knew that I would always be a student, yet I realized that it was time for me to take responsibility for being a teacher.

Everything in my life began to flow faster. My dreams were filled with even more color and richness and, what seemed to be, messages for me.

In one particular dream, a terrible fight broke out. The fight quickly escalated into a battle as guns began blazing and shots rang out everywhere. I ran for cover and tried to escape in a hail of bullets. Suddenly a strange man ran out ahead of me, taking shots that were clearly meant for me. He protected me from harm and virtually rescued me

In the morning, the meaning of the dream escaped me. But on a gut level, I felt a tremendous sense of protection. As the day progressed, I came to understand that this dream was sending me a message of assurance and safety. In this subtle way, someone was telling me that I would be protected in my travels.

I awoke on that beautiful sunny morning, after my dream of protection, and opened all the windows. I was filled with a sense of wonder and love, and a readiness to explore further and further.

The day flew by, with the kind of excitement that I usually feel when I pack for a wonderful trip. Anticipation and expectation filled me. That night, there was another tunnel dream, more words and another story drifted through the holes in time, coming to rest awkwardly in the present. After this day of sunshine, came *The Year of Light*.

8

FROM THE TIME TUNNEL:

The Year Of Light

I awakened. Slowly, very slowly, I became aware, aware of my body, aware of the room, aware of the light. I felt as if I had been dreaming for a long, long time, though I could remember no dream.

There was a feeling of heaviness. I couldn't feel any parts of my body, just a feeling of heaviness and heat. A glorious, sleepy heaviness seemed to permeate all the places I thought my body should be. A hot, heavy air seemed to rest on my face, pressing against me.

Slowly, I became more and more aware of my body, more aware of the pain and the heat. It seemed a strange effort to breathe, as if I'd just begun breathing for the first time, breathing a murky, heavy heat. I could feel this heat pass into my throat, creep through my chest and lungs. I felt it burning me, awakening me, giving me life.

My eyes felt too heavy to open. The lids felt like dry pieces of old paper, stiff and painful, hot. It was so hard to keep them open, it seemed a fight, like a weight was pushing against the brittle paper I called eyelids. But the paper began to have life, flickering life, opening with painful, burning, quick movements, opening to an intense, luminous, brilliant light.

Everything was stiff, hurt. I tried to raise myself up and the room was dizzying, turning in circles. It was a long, long time before it stopped.

I tried again to raise myself up and look down at my feet. A large, heavy piece of ceiling seemed to keep my right foot crushed to the floor. It was difficult to keep my body up and push at the weight at the same time. It seemed to take such a long time, and then freedom! It looked bruised and black, but I could move my foot. It didn't seem any more painful than the rest of me.

The room was so bright, it hurt, stung to keep my eyes open. I wondered why, the room seemed enclosed, except for the broken piece of ceiling, and there were no windows. And then the unfamiliarity of the room struck me. I had no remembered awareness of this place. Nothing looked like I had ever seen it before. I had no idea where I was!

Then, a worse fear, a terrible dread started deep within me and electrified my whole being with fear. I had no idea who I was! I was shocked, my heart was pounding through my chest. I felt sick and deeply afraid. I tried to calm myself. Who am I? Where am I? And what has happened to me?

The thought, that I must have hit my head, seemed to calm me. Obviously I have lost consciousness and at any moment, everything will come rushing back to me.

I took a deep, deep breath and got up, took a few steps. "I can still walk." Relief. I felt calmer. I felt very unsteady on my feet, weak, but now fully awake, a little stronger.

The room looked strange. It was fairly empty but the little that was there, was strewn about everywhere. Empty boxes, empty bottles, old pieces of blankets and some furniture that looked like it had been picked up and thrown across the room with force. There was an outside door that looked like it had been bolted from the inside. Had I done that? I hobbled up to the door and unbolted the thick bar. I tried to pull the door open but it seemed stuck, so heavy, it took every drop of energy and all the will I had, to open it.

What I saw outside was a total blinding light like I had never seen before. It was like staring into an intense, white flame. I dropped the door and it shut quickly. I rubbed my eyes and everything looked red, on fire. In the room, everything looked double. My eyes burned with heat. I was stunned.

I sat on one of the legless chairs for a long time. The room slowly began to seem darker and more comforting. My mind was starting to wake up but I felt very tired and at a loss.

The heat of the light seemed to have entered my throat and I felt an intense thirst. I found a bottle filled with a strange smelling liquid, which I quickly drank. I felt hungry but every bottle left seemed empty. I tore through everything left in the room. I went through every bottle, box and jar. Only one jar contained a few drops of something that smelled familiar, smelled sweet. My mouth recognized the little honey left in the jar and I licked, as far as my tongue could stretch. I pushed my fingers deep inside every part of the jar I could reach and I licked my fingers until long after there was any taste left.

I didn't know what to do next, I felt so tired. I laid down on the hot floor and fell asleep with my fingers inside my mouth.

I woke up all at once and had the immediate thought that it must be noon, it was so bright; and then I remembered.

I felt better than I had. I felt awake and hungry, and with dismay, I looked around the room. I didn't know who I was, or where I was, or what had happened, but I knew I couldn't stay here. I had to leave and find food and water!

I opened the door and was blinded, again, by the intensity of the light. I forced my eyes to stay open but I could see nothing. I stepped outside and I could still see nothing. The ground looked gray, hot and bare. Everything else was light, as far as I could see. I went back inside and sunk into the dark floor.

I wondered if there was some great fire burning in the distance, out of control, so great a fire it could light the sky for a million years. "*Where am I,*" screamed in my head, for a long, long time!

After a while, panic does indeed burn itself out and I was ready for some kind of action. If I walked out in this heat, how would I manage to see and keep walking? And I had to go out there. I had to find food, help.

I looked through everything in the room carefully. "There's nothing in this damn place!" I settled for what was left of an old jacket, tied it around my head, letting it hang partly in front of my eyes. It didn't matter anymore. I took one last look at the closed door behind me, my heart filled with fear, and then I took my first step.

It was a long time before I looked back and when I did, I could see nothing. Every direction looked the same. I seemed lost in some luminous haze. It was too disorienting to look in any direction but up ahead. I found if I kept my head down and my eyes focused on the ground, I could stand the intense light and keep moving onward.

It was not as hot as it had, at first, seemed, but I could feel the heat from the sky on the back of my neck and I was grateful for the long, thin sleeves on my tired, stiff arms. I stopped once in a while to rest but it was too fearful to stop. I kept going.

I felt like I had been walking forever. I lost what little sense of time I had at first had. It seemed as if my mind had stopped. Had I been walking hours, days, minutes? I had no idea and no reason to want to know.

When my legs finally stopped, I was forced to stop. I laid down on the ground, my body aching, and my mind started again.

I may have slept, dreamed, I don't know, but I awakened to a nightmare. The sky was still white, hot, shining. It seemed to reflect everywhere, even to making the dirt under my feet shine with intensity.

I started off again, even though a new darkness crept over my heart, into my soul. I was filled with despair. I couldn't stop the thoughts. There was no sun that I could see in the sky, no traces of a fire in the distance. Only a dark gray dirt everywhere, reflecting a ghost of a white mist. I didn't know how long I could keep going. I didn't know if I wanted to keep going.

With every step, the light seemed to take shape and become a ghost screaming at me. "You are the only one alive. Walk as far as you can, but I am the only one you will ever see." I ran until I couldn't move. I may have slept,

I don't know. I lost touch with what it means to sleep and be awake.

I found myself lying face down in the dirt, the feeling of my nose being filled with the dust of the earth. I think I may have cried, but I don't know. My consciousness and body seemed to have broken away from each other, to sadly separate and become pieces of confusion, resting in the dirt.

I turned over and faced the sky, opening my eyes wide, wanting to lose any final piece of myself. To my surprise I found it was easier, my eyes did not immediately close with pain. The tight, dry skin around my eyes, eased up a little. It seemed a little less bright.

I kept going for an eternity. I was able to look up at the sky and around me now, and my eyes felt rested, in an easy squint. What was happening? Was this supposed to be night? Night should have happened three days ago. Did it matter? I was the only person left alive, anyway. There was not one sign of life, anywhere that I had seen or sensed, not a tree, not a bird, not even an ant. I prayed to see an ant.

I walked for such a long time. I couldn't decide if I was dead or alive, but the argument kept me going. Ahead, I thought I saw something move. I couldn't tell what, until I got closer. When I saw what it was, I ran and threw my face into the murky, black-white pool of water I had stumbled upon, gasping for life. The feeling of wetness in my throat, on my face, in my eyes, was a feeling so sweet, I will never forget.

I had a feeling then, that something wanted me to live; it may only have been luck wanting me, but it would do. I kept walking, walking into future days of unsurpassed terror, days of torture. The torture was so great at every moment, I felt I could not keep going. I tried to find hope, but there was little. I could see clearly, most of the time. It was painfully bright but I could now, at least, look.

But there was nothing to see. The old ghost yelled in my head, "You're the only one who lives."

There was water in my brittle body and I could still walk. I could still walk into the nothingness the world had become. But I couldn't stand it much longer.

And the light became nothing compared to the silence surrounding me, screaming at me every moment. There was not one sound left in the world. The light and heat made no sound. No bird chirped, nothing moved, nothing breathed. There was no voice. I could not even hear the sound of my own breathing. Silence echoed through every bone in my body. Silence screamed into my soul.

I know now, I could stand to live without ever knowing myself, who I was. I could stand to live in any form of darkness. I could even face the light. But this long silence had become a knife in my heart I couldn't live with. I prayed for the end to come quickly.

I awakened to find the hallucination of something pulling me, poking me. I was shocked to feel, and more surprised to open my eyes and find a child, with her hands on my face. The shock pulled me to my feet screaming. But the child just stared at me. I asked her name. When I spoke, she met me with vacant looks. I realized, then, she couldn't hear or speak. The world was more silent than it had ever been. But this beautiful child was alive and because she was able to see, I was alive too!

We kept walking in the direction my *child of light* pointed to, and then the world seemed to turn from gray-white haze to a gray-green earth.

We reached a hill she clearly wanted to cross. When we reached the top, I looked out at a small village in the distance. And as we ran together, hand in hand, down the hill, I began to hear life. An unequaled joy filled my being. I could hear a stream in the distance, and the great beauty of human voices.

The first person we met said, "Who are you?" I said, "Mea." She said, "Welcome." And I knew that the year of light was over. The next year, 3014, would be a year of sound and music.

9

Reflections On The Year of Light

The Year of Light was nothing less than an assault on my senses. As Mea told her story, my body ached with a battered stiffness and my eyes smoldered. I not only felt the bodily pain but I also experienced the agonizing terror in her mind. In hearing and writing her story, I wandered through the hot, barren landscape of her experience, not knowing at all where she or her story were headed.

I came to yearn for some sign of life, hoping that something would crawl out from under her words and scurry across the luminous gray dust in my mind. I could feel my other senses reach out further, in the absence of sound, though my ears still strained with hope.

I wondered, as she wondered, what could possibly have happened to her world? Had there been a nuclear war or accident, or maybe some kind of ecological disaster was playing itself out. No answers ever came, only endless questions and speculations.

In the end, there was hope of a sort. I felt Mea there with me, thankful and longing to share with me that feeling of hope, that moment of hope stirred by the sounds of life and living. And I couldn't help but think of all the sounds that I disregard in my haste and hurry.

I opened my ears, with delight, to hear the music of life in all its richness. I began to listen closer to the sounds of life, its cries and calls, its dusty squeaks and velvet whispers. I began to hear, with new ears, all the beautiful sounds of this world. I knew that these sounds were the sounds of hope.

Sometimes I feel very frightened for our Mother Earth, frightened that in our complacency, we will destroy her and all the life that she sustains. Mea's story brought that fear to the surface again. Yet as I looked more closely at my fears, I was forced to think about the nature of life and the hope that life provides. Life is the chance, the opportunity, to learn the peculiar lessons and revelations of this world, this planet and this dimension. While there is life, there is hope for this learning and these lessons.

The sounds of living things seem so much more like music to me now. Perhaps as we stop to listen to this music, we take the first small step towards saving ourselves and our opportunity to learn.

Only a few days after *The Year of Light*, while still listening closely to the world, I had another tunnel dream, told to me by a man named Henri. He stood by me at the typewriter and whispered into my mind each word of his painful, yet beautiful story. Here then is Henri's story, which he calls, *A Better Life.*

10

FROM THE TIME TUNNEL:

A BETTER LIFE

Henri never walked anywhere. Instead, he always seemed to pace. A stiffness seemed to hang in his body, a pressure unseen, a pressure unfelt.

He was in a very bad mood on this cool morning. Anyone could tell by watching him, which was unusual. Henri had carried his bad mood within him for a long time, for years, but it was always controlled, an uncomfortable vapor, always swelling and contained within his chest, a cloud of thick air, constricting his body, stiffening his steps and his mind.

To look at him, he appeared to be a man of strength, discipline, control and purpose. And on this cool morning, Henri was struggling to remain a man of purpose.

He had risen early, long before sunrise, and left the shelter, anxious for this lonely walk, anxious to free himself and start on his journey back home. He paced through his usual miles, walking until he reached the cliffs, walking into the quiet, broken only by him, stillness broken only by his steps and the voices inside his head. Voices, he was used to always ignoring. Voices, that told him about feelings, feelings he was used to controlling.

He sat on the cliffs for a long time, just staring, staring at the sky, staring coldly at his own feelings, until the stagnant vapor seemed to swell through his body, and building up, to break through, coming out in force, all at once, a very cold flood of tears.

He cried violently, with despair, the cool tears feeling like ice on his cheeks. And then it was over. It had felt strange to cry. It was time to go back to the shelter, and prepare for his journey. He had no remembrance of when he had ever cried before, and it was easy to lock these tears away too. As he walked away from the cliffs, a finger seemed to quickly touch his shoulder, a finger of icy wetness. With a chill, he turned quickly to face emptiness and he wondered if someday he would remember this emptiness and his tears. And then, with a slow toss of his head, he laughed and he was on his way.

The day of remembrance did come, many, many years later, long years, filled with eternity. Henri sat on a different cliff and he remembered his life. He reviewed his past and remembered, with sorrow, the tears of that day. That had been the second time in his life he had cried. The first time had been a long time before that, when Henri had been quite young.

He sat there remembering that first time, seeing the faces in front of him, picturing exactly how they all looked. Everything flashed in front of him. He remembered his mother's beautiful face, a face filled with life and feelings and bravery. She looked so brave. Thinking back now, I think I was the only one, the only one who ever saw her tears. I remembered, my father never saw them.

I'm not sure why he couldn't. To me, they were startling, so out of place. Her face always shone, shone with happiness, with feeling and with light.

The few times I've ever seen her unhappy, her eyes became dark, dark pools that seemed to be filled with a very deep water, water that she kept in place there, letting only one tiny drop escape to drift slowly down and rest precariously on her beautiful cheekbone, like a diamond glistening in all directions, crying out to be seen, but holding back bravely. Her face remained still, but filled with a deep emotion.

I felt a little guilty, even then, we had been so close. But my father always said, '"Your mother is a woman of feeling. She refuses to look at the real world. She doesn't understand courage. It's up to us men to go on with the work of the world, to ignore the feelings and do what has to be done, to go on with our purpose."

Even if that means leaving, leaving my home, family, planet and the light of my beloved mother? I listened to my father. I left then, and I never felt anything again, except what I thought was courage. I went on with our purpose, the mission.

There has been so much arriving and too many departures on the many journeys since, but none, not one, ever brought me back to my beautiful home planet and that beautiful face.

I had always accepted my work, I think with my father's courage. But I never felt the purpose he felt, at least not until I met Galle. When I arrived on her planet, it reminded me so much of my home. And I think, now, Galle's face reminded me of my mother's face. The features were very different but the same light was there, shining from her eyes. Though I had not really started feeling yet, then, only remembering a little.

Galle and I were soon joined and we had two peaceful years together before I was assigned a new position and we were sent on our journey, a journey that would change our lives.

I was excited from the first. Or should I say, it was the first time in my life I felt such excitement. The planet Earth had always intrigued me. It was a planet of my ancestors. My very name, Henri, was an Earth name, handed down from a great grandfather of long ago. As a child, I had been fascinated with Earth and longed to go there.

I considered myself lucky. There were many problems with journeying to Earth but my ship would be the first one to attempt the crossing in over a hundred years. It was the only assignment that had excited me in years. I couldn't wait to get started!

I was glad, at first, that Galle had been okayed to join us. I was very proud of her medical training and because we had not been getting along lately, I thought the journey would be good for her.

Galle had been becoming more and more difficult, lately. When we spent time together, she complained constantly that I worked too hard, I didn't spend enough time with her. When we were together, it made me want to be working. She, herself, seemed to be losing interest with her medical studies and work, even though I constantly urged and encouraged her. I didn't know her anymore. I wondered when the light had left her eyes. Soon I forgot I had ever seen it there. After that, preparation and work, getting ready for the journey, totally consumed me.

The journey was more difficult than any of us ever imagined it would be. When we finally arrived, it was much later than we had expected. It was late in the Earth year of 3709.

The journey had taken much out of all of us, and more out of our equipment. The damage had been great to our ship and it was unclear if we could ever travel in it again. We had planned on the usual contact with our planet during the trip and once on Earth. We had been so proud of our technology that would enable us to always remain in contact, but many of our precious instruments were destroyed. I knew then that Center Control would assume we perished. I couldn't face the fact that it was doubtful that the necessary repairs could be made, and contact might, never again, be possible with Center Control.

Galle had been very little help to me during our journey turned into ordeal. I rued the day I had begged her to embrace her responsibility and come with me. Of the eight crew members, she was the only one I wished we had left behind. And Galle wished for that too.

The time, after our arrival on Earth, was a difficult one. It was a time of healing and repairing, building and exploring. We were prepared to build small shelters, and, in the weeks following the crash, we kept busy with this and the repair of our ship.

We started making plans to explore the planet in the future, when we were all rested and well and had our simple shelters built. We knew people were alive on Earth somewhere, but because of much of our equipment failure, we had no knowledge of where we were, in relation to any other beings who might be sharing the planet with us. We had no idea where we had landed, other than that we had reached Earth.

Everyone decided that we must feel hopeful. We could survive for a very long time with the supplies we had left on the ship. We had plenty of time to find food and explore the planet. Everyone decided that we must draw on our strength and build up our spirits. Galle said, "I feel our new home is going to be a better life for all of us. Don't you feel it!" Everyone held hands and agreed. "We will all be happy here!"

As each day passed, I began to hate our new life more and more. I laughed at myself, the excitement I had felt at the prospect of this journey, so long ago. What a fool! Now I would never get the promotions I richly deserved. I would never get the rewards of all my hard work. My important career was over. I might never see Central Control again. Why had this happened to our ship? We had the finest ship and equipment available. We should have made it to this Earth safely, and been able to leave.

And worst of all, no one but me seemed interested in finishing repairs and leaving for home. I didn't understand any of them and I had somehow lost control over them. They were all excited and Galle decided she really loved this new planet. I hated this planet Earth!

I spent most of my time alone, working on the ship, working on repairs with a vengeance. I couldn't wait to leave, even though I knew no one else would be going with me. They said I was a fool.

The day finally came when I felt we were ready. The ship was functioning and I knew we could make it. My former crew said the ship was still too damaged to attempt the long trip; I would never make it, what was wrong with me. The only thing that was wrong with me was that I couldn't wait for a rescue from home. I knew there wouldn't be one for a long, long time, if ever. I also knew, that there was nothing more that any of us could do for our ship. The only thing left for me, was the attempt. And I had the courage to make it, to make the attempt alone.

I was ready, wound up, and waiting for the dawn. Soon the ship would lift off and away and I couldn't wait to go, to get away. I paced beside the ship, waiting for dawn and the Galle I used to know, who would arrive soon.

She came to say good-bye. "Please Henri, don't do this. You don't have a chance, you must know that!" I looked at her coldly and said nothing. "Why? Why are you doing this?" Galle screamed at me. "Please Henri, we have a chance to build a good life for ourselves on this planet! We can make it a beautiful life, a better life, all of us together! Why won't you even try?"

I really didn't want to talk to Galle any longer. "I can't wait to go back to our life and our work. You've never understood my work; you've never understood responsibility, or you'd be on that ship with me."

"You're right, I don't understand your responsibility, or why you've let it make you miserable all these years. But I do understand that our lives should be filled with love. Stay and find it with me Henri. We can make a new start." Her voice was alive, begging. "Please, I love you Henri. I want you to stay." And she reached out to me, her hands shaking with emotion, arms reaching, reaching for me. But I was too far away. I wanted to spit on her trembling fingers. Instead, I spit on her heart. "I can't wait to leave you and this stinking planet!"

And then I was on the ship, pulling the controls, starting her off, filled with my old sense of purpose.

It surprised me, but I was afraid to take one last look out at "beautiful Earth," so I forced myself to. They were all out there, the people I started this miserable journey with. They hadn't the courage to come with me, only to say good-bye. They were all there, some of them feebly waving at me, spineless fools. I was surprised to see so many of them crying, but not Galle, she wasn't crying. She waved strongly, bravely, and as I pulled out, she ran towards the ship, smiling, giving me her sign for "I love you."

And her shiny face was the last thing I saw on Earth. The one tear resting on her cheekbone, glistened and seemed to shoot up to the sky, and follow me. It reminded me of something, someone, from a long time ago.

And I was off, flying through a whirling vortex of sky and powerful emotion.

I opened my eyes to a very dark sky, a very dark planet. I was dazed. I had no idea where I was, who I was. Yes, it took a long time to figure out what had happened to me, and many dark years to figure out who I was.

I thought of myself as "Henri the fool," in those days. And I kind of enjoyed the thought.

I estimated it had been at least two Earth years since the crash. And I was grateful for that crash. I had long ago realized that when my ship had crashed before reaching home, a part of me had crashed with it and died, exploding and exposing a part of me I hadn't known or wanted to know before. I think it was my heart.

I still couldn't remember how long I had journeyed before the fire started on my ship. I only remembered that strange relief I felt when I knew I would crash. It was a relief to feel that final sense of helplessness; and I let go, and fell completely and out of control. It didn't feel like I was going to die in that dark sky; it felt like I was being born.

I spent the next years roaming this new planet that fate had placed me on, had saved me for. And that thought made me want to do everything I could for the planet.

And so I began to know myself and to learn how to feel, though feelings had begun for me the moment of the crash, feelings for this planet that had cushioned my painful hurtling away from a dark life, a planet that seemed to have welcomed my cold body, brought it to life, and slowly and lovingly warmed it, through the years.

I had long since stopped wondering what planet I was on; I only wondered and wished to know if I shared it. The emptiness, the quiet, had turned into peace for me, but my new heart longed for another heart, a hundred hearts, to experience this beautiful planet with.

And one day I learned what a full heart meant. I met a beautiful, old woman on the road. And she was not to be the only human to share my new world; for she lived in a small house within a day's walking distance of a village.

I rested for a while in her house and we shared the best meal I've ever tasted. But I hadn't been prepared for the shock, when she told me the name of the planet I had roamed now for years. When the shock wore off, we told stories of our travels, of our lives, and we smiled and laughed. She told me stories of the village I was to visit the next day, stories of the people. The story I liked best, was one about a strong, beautiful medicine woman, with light in her eyes.

I couldn't wait to get to the village the next day. I was finally ready for a better life.

11

LOVE AND FEAR

Henri's story flowed easily from his world to mine. I could feel his life's journey flow too, in a full circle of transformation. At the end, I cried with joy and release. Henri paused in his dictation, to mark the story's end, and then said, "When you open your heart, you always do find ahead of you a better life."

I was amazed, once again, at how the process of receiving these stories was so much more than merely hearing words or seeing pictures and scenes. I could feel Henri's descriptions of places and feelings, as though his words and pictures could convey the fullness of emotions and sensations.

When Henri showed me his mother and spoke of his feelings for her, I could feel what she was like and I could feel his deep love and admiration for her. As he spoke of his father and his father's beliefs, I could feel his father's distance and a kind of unsettling contempt for emotions. As Henri drew away from his mother, I could sense his drawing away from a powerful part of himself and I could feel the cold emptiness that, like a vapor, rose in his chest.

I felt almost as if I could sense where these people were in their lives' journeys. I could feel their struggles with intellect and emotion, freedom and duty, love and fear. I felt Henri, moving through his life's journey, confused about his role and purpose in life, especially as it was defined by his father and society.

Henri expressed the deep conflict inside that arose between his feminine and masculine qualities, the yin and yang, a conflict that became a full scale war. I could feel Henri trying to resolve this conflict, control it, deny it and finally trying to run from it.

As Henri hurtled through space, in his reckless attempt to escape love and his own heart, he began to sense how lost and alienated he had become. Henri felt a sense of relief as he began to lose control. He felt both the pain and ecstasy of exposing his heart, and for the first time in a long time, he felt truly alive.

Henri's transformation may seem to be quick, almost instantaneous, but it wasn't. Henri communicated to me, not so much in words but in long deep feelings, that the years spent on this planet of refuge and respite were years of gradual healing and change. The crash was just the beginning, a chance to begin again.

As the planet nurtured him, held him safely, there seemed to be a peace forming slowly inside. I could feel Henri's warmth and wholeness and how, in opening his heart, he did find a better life.

12

ALARA

The night of August the 18th, only a few days after finishing *A Better Life*, I went to bed for a good night's sleep. Rick and I talked for a short while until he dropped off to sleep, somewhere in the middle of a sentence.

There was a light cool breeze coming in the window that blew the shade back and forth. The sounds of crickets flowed in on waves, until the calls seemed to come from every corner of the room. I felt suspended in a sea of sound, on a cloud of *buzzes* and *whirs*. As I listened longer to the crickets, the sounds seemed to vibrate into my body. I slowly felt the tingle in every muscle and bone, and as the vibrations grew stronger and filled my body, I felt like I would almost disintegrate.

Bathed in this beautiful sensation, I opened my eyes to see a luminous sparkle of tiny lights and a movement of color in the air. Very often, when my spirit guides wish to contact me, I can sense their presence by this display of sparkling colored lights in the darkened room.

My guides usually either speak to me, their words plainly and clearly entering my mind, or they communicate through the symbols and images of the dream state. They speak either to my conscious or unconscious mind, depending on the nature of the message or lesson they want to give to me.

On this particular night, I didn't hear any message coming through, so I assumed that there would be a dream. I awoke early that morning with fragments of that dream still ringing in my mind.

I sat at my typewriter, later that day, and the story that began in my dream slowly unfolded. I was immediately startled as I discovered that Alara was the narrator of this story.

I guess I really thought that after *The Gardens of Rio*, I had accepted the idea that Alara was my future self, or a part of me that already existed in the future. I remembered being quite upset at first, and then slowly adjusting my beliefs until I could at least accept the possibility. But as I heard Alara speaking in my ear, as I felt her familiar rhythms and warm vibrations, my head began to spin again with the shear immensity of the reality.

I was beginning to see that, prior to this, I must have only accepted Alara intellectually, like an idea in a book, interesting, fascinating. But as a living presence in my life, speaking to me, telling me of my future, she was overwhelming!

I typed the words that Alara spoke to me, but I was clearly in another world the whole time. My next surprise came when the story stopped, rather abruptly, very soon after it started. Perhaps I was being given an opportunity to sit with the concept of Alara. I gladly accepted the time and space in which to think about Alara, her presence and her intimate relationship to me.

I drifted through the remainder of the day, trying to understand and accept Alara more completely, and preparing myself for the writing of this most personal tale.

That night I dreamed vividly and clearly about Alara. She seemed so close to me, so like me, and yet different in many ways. I was fascinated by the feeling. Alara was discovering me in her travels through time, finding parts of herself rooted in me. And I was discovering Alara, truly seeing the ways in which she was a distant extension of me.

I awoke with a deeper understanding of myself and my relationship to Alara. I also felt I could see further into the nature of time and change. I began to see life as something always becoming and identity as something always unfolding. These ideas weren't new to me on an intellectual level. My meeting with Alara helped me to understand these concepts on a more emotional and soul level.

I meditated on the *dream* for quite a while, when all of a sudden, I felt an odd urge. I opened my eyes and felt compelled to climb out of bed and walk to my bedroom mirror. I was strangely excited as I walked quietly on the carpeted floor. I felt as if I were being told to look into the mirror. I hesitated, momentarily frightened, unsure. I faced the mirror and focused my eyes.

I looked deeply into my eyes and for a long moment, I saw someone else looking back. The moment stopped, frozen in time; Alara peered back at me from behind my eyes, and then she was gone. For all the developing warmth between her and me, I felt a chill in that passing moment. I felt the starkness of something made, all too suddenly, real.

During the following week, I often thought of Alara, and occasionally felt her near, but I didn't find a moment to sit at my typewriter and let her story continue. This was a very busy period for me, and the *real world* of business and survival called to me, all too often. Rick and I were just weeks away from opening our new hypnotherapy practice and there were furnishings to find and endless supplies to order. Ten days passed before I was able to continue with my writing.

It was early evening. I sat down, put my fingers on the keys and the story resumed as though only a few seconds had passed. I couldn't believe my eyes as I watched the seamless continuity, not a thought or a word lost.

The story proceeded a little further and when the night was over, I had ventured deeper into the heart of the tale. I knew that I wouldn't be able to write again for days and it made me sad and impatient. It almost seemed, in this writing process, that I was wandering down deeper into the twists and turns of some magical canyon, never knowing what was around the next turn or in the next cavern. Then abruptly, I would make camp and stay there for days, excited, anxious, waiting to continue the journey. It was difficult to leave the stories for any length of time and camp on that plateau waiting, but sometimes I just had to.

On September 8th, Rick and I officially opened our private practice. The preceding week had been full of cleaning, painting, arranging and rearranging. We were very proud to have created such a relaxing, peaceful, plant-filled office within the tight confines of our budget. Tired and satisfied, we sat down to dinner that evening and talked on and on of how our dreams were coming to fruition.

After dinner, I had every intention of just relaxing or reading in bed, but my curiosity got the best of me and I ended up at the typewriter once again. The story flowed like a stream in a spring rain. Picking up exactly where she had left off, Alara resumed the spinning of her magic tale. She never seemed impatient or hurried and yet, she was bursting with excitement and very pleased to be with me writing again. Alara told her story with energy and grace, like a dancer dancing. Sometimes her energy seemed boundless. There were areas of difficulty, where she introduced very complex ideas and unique perspectives, but Alara tried patiently to illustrate and clarify.

Somewhere around midnight, I finished typing a particularly difficult section of the story and knew that I was tired and ready for sleep. I also sensed that I needed a few days to ponder Alara's words and thoughts. This story of Alara's was becoming a challenge on many levels.

September quickened its pace as our business increased. I tried to set aside time for Alara's story but I often had to alter my schedule. When I did find time to write, it was often only a brief time. In this piece-meal manner, I finally finished Alara's story, *Everlasting Love,* on October 15th, almost two months in the making.

Before you read Alara's story, prepare yourself for some challenging ideas. Once again, try to temporarily suspend your beliefs and at least entertain these broad concepts, foreign as they may seem. Forgive yourself for perhaps not immediately grasping everything in its entirety. I struggled long and hard with this story. I found myself reading and re-reading some sections, and in the end, still not comprehending fully.

Sometimes I think that the ways in which we describe reality, in terms of time, space, life, death, reincarnation, hereafter etc., are only child-like metaphors, only simplistic nursery rhymes that lightly sketch a greater truth that lies far beyond our ability to truly understand. The deeper truth that transcends descriptions and metaphors, that life and love are eternal, is at the heart of *Everlasting Love.*

13

FROM THE TIME TUNNEL:

EVERLASTING LOVE

It was a time of powerful emotions. The planet had been set on fire and it seemed like no leader, no country, no church and no individual knew how to put the fire out; and in the years before, after and during 2097, everyone was busy trying.

In June of that year, Maura was basically alone, her world too busy for her, caught up in its own activity, and Maura was a little too young yet for the world. She would turn seventeen at the end of June, and she was only beginning to see where she would fit in, only beginning to feel where she wanted her place to be in her world. There were glimmers of ideas and beliefs, and already the glimmers were beginning to have a certain shine and strength that seemed to get a little stronger with each new day in her life.

Maura was a girl of dreams, an artist, and a girl becoming a woman in a different world. A woman with not only a great talent but a woman with love in her heart was coming alive and I had the good fortune to be part of, and to watch, this new birth.

I first met Maura on June 1st of 2097 and in one day, we became friends, great friends. We became friends on a glorious, beautiful, sunny day in June and we were friends through many lifetimes of sun, rain and fire.

The sun in the park was catchy. I could feel it tickling my bare arms and legs and reaching up further in, to tickle my mind. The sun slowly began to warm the tiredness out of my body and to softly brush the gloominess in my mind away.

I had just returned from a very long journey; my body ached with weariness and my mind was filled with troubled thoughts. I had left part of myself behind, in another place, with different people. But this sun was starting to win; I let go, staring at its fire and it began to warm me and bring me back.

I still half wondered why I had allowed Francis to talk me into coming to this park today. I was certainly not an expert on art, as much as I loved it.

"Well, I'm here, so I guess I might as well enjoy this." As I moved through the green life surrounding me, I began to become involved in the experience, indeed the luxury, of gazing at art among trees, a luxury I had not experienced for a long time. I drifted among the trees slowly, lazily enjoying the beautiful works of art represented.

Critiquing the art wasn't something I wanted to do. I listened curiously to the viewpoints of the judges and I was glad that my part would be, not to judge, but to choose. I decided not to choose from my mind but with my heart.

Francis had asked me three months ago, to attend this art event and to pick one work to be exhibited at our annual gala. I think at the time I thought this trip would force me to take a break from my work. I know Francis thought so. Of course, now, here I was, the time had come and I was not much in the mood for a break. All I could think of was work. There was so much to be done, I had even called Francis earlier. "There are several people in the area I know would be happy to do this Francis. I'll just come back to the project."

"Alara, what do I have to do to get you to take a rest? Maybe I should make it a rule, six months on the project, and six months off."

"Six months! That would be unbearable, impossible!" I was afraid to complain anymore, for fear he would make it a rule. So I realized, finally, it was time for a break and time for an art show.

An hour after I arrived, I forgot there was anywhere else in the world I wanted to be. The morning and the park were exhilarating and I became caught up in their beauty. I became totally involved in the choosing of one special work of art.

I had almost finished going through the exhibits, when I realized I was torn between two pieces. The first one was a sculpture of the universe by a noted artist of the planet. The other, a pre-modern oil, reminded me a little of a Monet that I had once seen in Paris, during one of my trips for the project. I think that's why it appealed to me. It reminded me of a Paris that once had existed, a world where people appreciated art.

And then another exhibit stopped me, startled me. When I saw it I knew, I knew immediately, it was the one. A painting beautiful enough to symbolize a gala.

It was magnificent and perfect, all at once. The colors created on the canvas, were like no others. They had a clearness and wildness not seen in the passionless world we live in. I felt it was the most beautiful painting I had ever seen.

I was so taken with it, that no one else's opinion mattered to me. One of the judges really thought I should go with the sculpture. "It's much more fitting. The painting by Micalo shows lots of talent but not enough technique; it shows a wonderful use of color and I would like to see what this artist, Micalo, is doing a few years from now, but the work needs more development. It's not ready yet. Go with the sculpture, Alara. It's much more what you're looking for." I hadn't known what I was looking for, that day, but somehow I knew I had found it.

The oil was entitled simply, "LOVE," and I was going to make sure it was hanging at the center for this year's gala. At first, I was surprised to find that no one knew much about this painter, Micalo. An Unknown? A beginner even, perhaps? Then, I realized that only a new artist would create something as refreshing, so full of fire.

I couldn't wait to make the arrangements. I couldn't
wait till Francis saw it. Would he like it? He'll probably
say, "You're crazy as usual, Alara, but I love it!"

I was so in love with the painting itself, I couldn't wait
to meet its creator. I was curious. People would say,
"Passion like this has never been seen before. Who would
paint like this?" And I wanted to know.

Micalo had not been able to attend the art show so it
was arranged for us to meet at 3:00 that afternoon. I was
surprised, a little, to find out that Micalo was a woman and
a student. I just couldn't wait till 3:00. I was looking forward, with great excitement, to meeting my new discovery. I was so eager, I arrived at quarter of three to find a
young and pretty girl waiting for me.

Maura Micalo was just a few days short of seventeen
and just as fresh and beautiful as her painting. We hit it off
immediately. After the first ten minutes of her appreciation
for my choosing her work and my appreciation of her
work, we both seemed to take a deep breath and to stop. It
was funny, but it only seemed to take a moment for Maura
to realize that I was not just the project director of Cross,
whose taste in art would change her life, and I in turn saw
not just a young, struggling artist, but a kindred spirit in
our world, a very familiar woman I knew I already liked. It
only seemed to take a moment for us to become friends.

It had gotten into a habit, every afternoon at three,
Maura and I would meet at our favorite place, the gazebo.
We would spend hours over tea, talking about art, life, the
world and ourselves. Maura agreed with the ideals of
Cross and was excited to find them in our world. She
seemed to understand, in the core of her being, what Cross
was trying to do. She was thrilled to find a whole organization to believe in, and one person who knew her and
believed in a world she, too, wanted desperately to believe
in. Maura was excited that her oil had been chosen for
Cross. I knew she didn't really quite believe it yet. I wondered, then, how would it change her life, change her?

Maura, as yet, hadn't really tasted fame. I wondered
how she would like that flower of bitter sweetness. I won-

dered if she would take a deep breath and learn to thrive
on that pretty taste, and I wondered what that bouquet of
scented air would bring, into her now windless life. I made
a vow to watch her and if I ever saw her beginning to
choke on that bitter, compelling air of fame, I would step
in; I would be there for her. Oh, the innocent vows we
make in gazebos, on sunny warm days, in cold strange
worlds.

I knew Maura's core; I had felt it so clearly from that
very first look at her painting. The oil seemed to be everything Maura was, a simple beauty, a clear colorful energy,
and a purity so rare it seemed to stand out, to shock. Much
later, I decided that the purity was part of what attracted
the eye to the painting. It seemed to stand alone in the oil,
unprotected, reaching out to the gazer; it seemed to want
something. I know the oil scared people at times. It seemed
to shake their bones, softly, peacefully. And I knew why.

I had seen a lot of my world already, too much sometimes, I thought. That was why I was so happy to find
Maura's "LOVE". It was a perfect symbol. Inside the oil,
hiding, was part of what Cross stood for. One of our
desires was to nourish the art now left in the world. I think
"LOVE" showed people why. I think it shook them a little
and they began to understand. The beginning of an understanding was more than we hoped for; and that painting
by a young Micalo did that for us. The oil was a brilliant
contrast of a peaceful purity and a beautiful passion. The
painting showed us what was missing in our world.

I almost felt as if I had adopted Maura. She came into
my life so quickly. I guess we really did adopt each other.
There were no official papers passed, only quick, knowing
glances came from each other's souls and passed between
us on that first sunny day we met. Those glances signified
a pact that we were sisters and mothers and daughters and
friends. In just two weeks, my vacation had become a trip
home to be with my family.

June seemed to be turning out to be a very hot and lazy
month. I was now into my third week of vacation, and
thoroughly enjoying it, surprisingly enjoying my break

with the world. It was a time of rest for me, and introspection. A time my mind hadn't realized it needed but my soul welcomed. I had been working non-stop, for quite some time, as were most people involved in the project. We all felt that it was of the utmost importance. The world was in a terrible way and we felt our project, someday, could make a difference. That's not to say my work was not fulfilling on a daily basis. It was sometimes so fulfilling that it gave me the strength to keep going; it helped me keep my eyes open and not get blinded, as so many had. It allowed me to still be able to watch what our world was becoming and not turn away.

Project Cross was a research project massive in its scope. We knew that we might not see major results for a long time and we lived every day with the knowledge that results might come too late. But it did give us one thing, each and every day, that most of us felt we could no longer live without; something called hope.

I guess I should tell you a little about my work but it's not easy to explain. Especially since I really don't know who will be reading this, where you will be coming from, whether you will even be able to understand my words.

Perhaps this will be so simple for you, it will be like a funny little nursery rhyme that you will laughingly pass on to your children as you smile about times long ago, fairy tales that, even if you remember, seem so long ago, so far away, a different world, a world so different and so long ago that you can't remember if it was real or not. Yes it is a different world and a real one. I think that's one of the main problems, it is always too real. It was too real and very different, long ago. It's very different now and all too, too real. And it will be different again and that same vivid curtain of realness will still be there.

You may look at these words from a different place still. You may be in a world coming towards them, approaching them, and if so, they will probably look so far away to you that you can't catch up to their realness, so far away that if you try to get near and grasp the words, their realness dissolves, sifts through your mind to some other place and is lost. But I think if you are very still, you can feel a little of that dust sifting into your heart and in feeling it, you will understand a little of my words.

There are so many angles and places to watch these words from. I wonder where you are, where your world is, who you are, watching me?

Perhaps you will read this from one place and, later on, from another. Perhaps you are reading from many different and real places, all at once.

Hello, my name is Alara. There are, have been, and will be other names too; but I won't confuse you any more than I have already. Besides, in this world, I am only and all of Alara.

I like to think of myself as a *space channeler* and from where you are, I may look like a time traveler and that may be a good description for you to understand. It is my work and I am very good at it. Francis says I have a natural talent for it. I've done this kind of work from many different spaces and times. I guess I've done it, to some degree, on and off, for many lifetimes.

There are several of us here, in 2097, working as channelers for Project Cross. It is a project encompassing many different times and places and it seems like as we go along, it expands like time itself.

I am one of seven space channelers and I am also project director. As project director, I am very involved in making decisions about the various journeys all of the channelers make. I also work with the research department assigned to correlate the information that is received from all of us.

The basic work of each channeler is to journey to mostly predetermined sites and carry out predetermined research. The research can be of scientific, sociological and psychic nature. The sites we travel to are in different spaces and levels of existence, not all of it human existence. Some may find it easier to think of these journeys as going to the past, to the future and to different levels existing in my present. One of the main reasons for this research is to enable us to look at the present chaotic state of the planet

Earth from a larger view, so that the best steps can be taken at this time to try to insure the survival of our planet and the remaining people.

The very means of obtaining this research gives us a secondary purpose, one of experimentation in travel, space travel, or could I say multi-dimensional space travel.

The process by which this travel is possible could fill volumes of books and is still very much in the process of being refined through experimentation. There are few people on the Earth today who have enough skill to work as a channeler, so we are in the process of training new channels. It seems to take quite a lot of training and experience, on many different levels and times. Like most of the channels working today, I have been in the process of training for this position I have now, for many different lifetimes.

Our work at Project Cross is fairly well accepted here in 2097, by the people who are aware of us, though some people consider us only a big experiment. Some people are very curious about us and what we are doing. Much of our research is being assimilated and is not available to the public, and since most people don't really understand the scope of the project, they accept this.

I have known some people, however, who have not. They have considered me someone who might be able to give them all kinds of information, for profit, curiosity and their own self development, in some way.

Most people seem to understand my work, at least my friends seem to, and to appreciate the delicate nature of the work. Maura was like this, though she would always say, "I wish I could see what you see, Alara. I wish I could go to the places you go to and paint them." I wished she could too because I knew she would do them justice; she was a wonderfully gifted artist.

Maura turned seventeen and with every day that passed, her painting seemed to be developing rapidly. I finally went back to work but we kept in touch as much as we could manage.

Every time we did get together was a time for celebration; at last I had found a sister. Or should I say, once again I had found Maura. For out of an intense longing to know, I confess, I had already taken a trip back through time and found the place where our friendship had been born. I was able to visit some initial lifetimes where our sistership had not always been easy, and some golden times of sharing friends. There were lifetimes we had to leave without saying good-bye and some where we seemed to forget our bond and had no desire to say good-bye or hello. Being able to see some of this and the friendship we now shared again gave me such a wonderful feeling of awe of the great continuance of love.

The gala was a wonderful event, an electric event, where everyone involved in Project Cross allowed themselves to let go of the burdens we all shared, to turn away from the troubles of the universe for just one night and to allow ourselves to smile a little too easily, and to laugh a little too happily. It was a night we all needed.

Maura Micalo's "LOVE" was a huge success. People were hearing about this new genius of the art world and the opportunity to see one of her most talked about works, here at the gala, was very exciting.

Art was rare in our time. There weren't many people with the soul left to paint and so Maura was becoming a star. She had come to the gala at my invitation and it was an exciting night for her. She was growing up very, very quickly, and happily tasting the excitement of success. She brought Danny with her, a man she had met only a week ago, a man with whom, from all appearances, she had fallen in love. They both looked so incredibly in love, it was a joy to watch them both together.

Maura had no family and I was her only friend. And I had certainly seen the loneliness she carried with her. Tonight I saw no traces of that aloneness I knew had always burdened her. The new love in her eyes made me so happy, it was hard not to cry.

And I really liked Danny too. The first night I met him, it seemed as if the three of us had always known each other. I knew Danny felt it too. He called Maura and I "the twins" but it seemed like the three of us were family.

It seemed like, so quickly, it was over. We had looked forward to the gala for so long and then it was finally here, and then, so abruptly, it was gone.

And then months arrived and disappeared, and we left that night far behind us. The world was different every day and the happiness of that night grew less real.

I hadn't been able to see Maura and Danny for a year, but I had talked to Maura about six months earlier, and she sounded like that first painting of hers, personified. Every once in a while I read about how well she was doing, one great Micalo success after another.

Work and one long journey kept me further and further away. One year turned into two, and when we finally arranged a visit; it was two and a half years since I had seen Maura's beautiful smile. It was a great surprise to find it wasn't there any longer. Maura was almost twenty but she looked too much older. We had days being happy, seeing each other again, and it was days before I saw clearly where her unhappiness was coming from.

Danny seemed to have stolen her smile but for the life of me I couldn't figure out why. He seemed to still love her, I was almost sure of it, not that you could tell by his actions. He treated her terribly, coldly; but she was totally, completely consumed by love for him.

Mostly Danny avoided me. Strangely, I felt like he was glad to see me but that it troubled him that I was there. Maura pretended nothing was wrong. There had never been any secrets between us and we felt as close and comfortable as we always had. We would always be sisters and two and a half years wouldn't change that. I slowly began to realize that Maura herself had no idea that anything was wrong, otherwise I knew it would have been natural for her to tell me.

I stayed with Maura and Danny for one uneasy month. Danny avoided me more and more, both of them insisting that nothing was wrong. I was more and more confused. I couldn't get anywhere with Maura and one day it finally came to me. I realized that I would never hear from Maura, what was happening, because Maura herself, had no idea. She had locked a terrible secret away in her heart and thrown away the key, because she knew that to open that door would kill her. She had closed herself completely away from the pain in her heart and gone away; her eyes were vacant. The Maura I knew had left and I didn't know where to look for her.

Danny was gone too. He made himself pretty inaccessible to me and when I did try to see him, the pain in his face was too much for me.

The black shadows filling the house I had so happily looked forward to visiting started to cling to me also. I couldn't stand to watch the ghosts I loved any longer. I knew I had to leave; there seemed to be nothing I could do but go. So go I did. I said good-bye to Maura and saw the only life left in her eyes flicker as I left.

I arrived back at work too quickly, none of it seemed to be real to me. I couldn't seem to concentrate and I didn't know what to do about the black shadows that seemed to still follow me and force me to remember two people I loved so much.

One day I woke up and admitted to myself an idea that had been brewing in my mind since I had gotten back. I spent two days convincing myself not to do it but on the third day, I got up and walked through the window, a window that I knew would take me to Maura and Danny and, perhaps, bring them back.

I was there all too quickly and damn, I wish I had prepared more. I had not much idea where, exactly, I was, and I searched my mind for any memories of this time.

I found myself in front of a door of a small house, so the logical thing to do, it seemed to me, would be to walk in, and so I did. With fear in my chest, I walked into a kitchen and a world all at once shiny and new, familiar and strange. And a moment later, a woman walked in, very startled to find me in her kitchen; a stranger enters her world. "Who are you?" "The woman next door," was all I could think to say. "Well, I had no idea someone was

moving in, the place has been empty so long. Welcome …
sit down and I'll get us some tea."

Get us some tea she did, and more tea, as we talked on
and on. She was so readily friendly and after an hour sitting in her kitchen, she said, "I feel I've known you all my
life."

I knew her so well, I wanted to say more, but I only
listened as she told me about her hard life, and as she told
me about her on and off again relationship with her husband. I listened with tears. I didn't want to hear about the
fights and how he had left her. I didn't want to hear what
my friend's life had been like, in this horrible world of the
past. She and her husband had created unhappiness. I
didn't want to see the pain in those very pure eyes that I
now knew as Maura's.

What had happened? It seemed obvious, even then,
that she and her future Danny loved each other. "I think
we both have so much to learn," she said reflectively, into
her tea cup. And for one moment, I felt so clearly that all
she and her husband really had to learn was that they
loved each other. And that all important truth was something they would spend lifetimes looking for, working
through, learning through and eventually come to know.

I wondered if I would be there to see some future
Maura's eyes, finally filled with the love that only comes
from realization; and maybe she would see the same reflection in Danny's future eyes. Perhaps then, their eyes would
shine with a light even stronger, having been tested and
forged with fire. Some day, they would put down the
weapons and give up the fight, and their love would
become peaceful. Would their love survive until the day
they could make peace with it?

I wanted so much to tell her, to tell her happier times
were ahead. I felt it. But I also knew there would be more
bad times too. I had just come from one of them. She
showed me a picture of the vacant ghost who was her
husband. I knew it was time to leave them. It was too
painful to see them this way, in the past, but I couldn't face
them in my present world, not yet.

I decided to take one more trip before going back to the Maura and Danny I knew. With uneasiness and a heart I wasn't sure wanted to see anymore, I found myself in a beautiful park.

I wasn't sure anymore of my purpose. I only know that sometimes it's sadder, more futile to take the role of a friend; to watch when there's nothing you can do. I didn't know what to look for anymore and once more, I didn't know where I was.

It was a beautiful park I found myself in, so still and bright and hopeful. Was there an answer in this park? I thought I heard echoes of other times and I kept walking, not knowing where I was going. The answer came so swiftly it took my breath away.

They were so different, but so very real. I knew at a glance who they where, even though I would not know their names this time around. They were giggling, so happily oblivious to the rest of the world, so much in love. I had to smile; was Maura an artist now too? She was so happily carving a beautiful heart on the young tree in front of her. "This heart will last forever," she whispered. And as they started to carve their names, I walked away I wanted them to have their moment, so filled with love and happiness, alone, unobserved.

I walked through the park and away from their world, slowly. How many moments of love and too many moments of pain they had gone through together. Now I knew that there had been a happy time for them in the past. I had seen it and I felt ready to face the present. They had experienced at least one moment of love.

As I walked through the park, another woman passed me, the music from her radio gently flowing into my consciousness, "Want you in my life, girl to be my wife, everlasting love ... open up your heart, never be apart ... everlasting love ... ooh, in love forever ..."

I smiled, I hadn't heard that kind of music for a long time and it brought back rushes of memories, memories of a sunnier world, filled with music. I strolled back happily to my world, to find out how Maura's and Danny's song would end.

I came back to an ominous message from Danny, "Alara, come as soon as you can-Danny." When I arrived, I found it wasn't soon enough. She was gone. Her world had stopped spinning. I sat by her bed, in shock, and held her hand. I looked at her pale, beautiful face and I stared at her lifeless eyes. There could never be an answer. But I demanded one now from Danny. He showed me her last work of art, her suicide note. "Danny, I can't go on, I know you've stopped loving me, and I can't bear it. This will make it easier for you. Good-bye Danny, I love you, and say good-bye to Alara for me, and give her my "LOVE".

I turned to see a man with eyes filled with intense pain, regret. "You know how much I loved her, Alara, don't you! She was everything to me, my life, everything. I could never, and I will never stop loving her. She didn't understand. I guess I didn't give her the chance. I didn't know what to do. I'm dying, Alara, I've got the sickness. I was afraid to tell her, afraid it would kill her. I didn't know what to do … I thought if I turned away from her slowly it would be better. I knew she'd hate me for it, hate me for not telling her; but I thought it would be easier for her, I swear it, I never thought she'd do this and now … now I've killed her." He looked at me and I'm not sure what he wanted, forgiveness, comfort? I could only scream at him and I screamed for a long time, "Damn you Danny, I didn't even get a chance to say good-bye!" And then I ran.

In the days and weeks that followed, I thought a lot about love and why that beautiful and everlasting fire had to cause so much pain. But thinking didn't seem to give me any answers or any peace. I decided, at last, to take another look, one last look, at an already finished painting.

The tangled webs we weave are called life.
Why are some so simple, so easy, so intricately beautiful?
Why are some so tangled and frayed, so thin they break,
so thick they feel heavy, so tight they hurt?
Does the rain, glistening on the web, make it beautiful?

Do the drops of shiny wet cleanse?
Or will the spiders wash away?

Another day, another hour, another moment,
they mix together, and grow further and further away.

When I arrived in town it was just sunrise. I sat under a huge, old tree and watched a bronze ball of fire come up in the sky, to awaken a new world, a future world, I was seeing for the first time.

I walked slowly to the town, savoring this planet of hope. It seemed a beautiful place. There were trees and gardens with flowers rich enough to paint. And I found a mother there, holding, comforting a crying newborn little boy called Michael. And six months later, a little girl was born and her mother called her Danielle.

As I walked away from the town, I passed the tree where I had sat and watched the sun come up on this real and different world, that would bring hope, and both a new start and a continuance of old hearts for so many. I sighed. It's always so real and so different, but love always seems to be there, hiding in the webs, the only constant, the only everlasting, in a world of constant renewal and change.

I looked at the tree, and I could almost see them. Yes, someday, Danielle would paint this tree and they would both stand here and hug and giggle and wonder who the lovers were that had carved their names on this tree, so long ago.

I wished them peace this time around. This time I wouldn't stay to watch them, either. I had to go back to my time. There was someone there who needed my comfort, and he needed to know, too, about everlasting love. And besides that, I had a last gift to pick up, a painting I truly loved. And I knew, now, I didn't have to stay and say good-bye.

14

THE THEATER OF LIFE

Everlasting Love is a story of enormous scope, encompassing pieces of many lifetimes. Yet, for me, it was also very personal and, at first, I was more affected by the smaller, more personal elements of the story. Alara's presence was fascinating to me. I found it difficult, at first, to become absorbed by the story line because I kept thinking of Alara and her significance to me. I kept noticing her and her attitudes and comments, as though I were being distracted by my shadow or my reflection in a passing window.

Alara brought to me a new and deeper dimension of myself. To see Alara in the story and to hear her describe her life was, for me, to see some as yet unknown part of my life. As I read Alara's story, I discovered secrets about me, hidden in the folds and corners of ordinary moments and conversations.

My mother sometimes tells me stories of my own childhood, stories about events and circumstances that I can't quite recall. I try to remember being two or three years old and wearing a particular dress or saying something incredibly cute, but it's just too long ago, too far away. Yet I don't doubt my mother's memory. I know that I take these stories and include them in that larger description of who I am. Those events, though not in my memory, are a part of me.

In a similar way, Alara's stories contain a part of me that I can't quite remember. I listen to her, her feelings and observations, and I incorporate these future fragments of myself into that larger picture of me. I began to see that becoming whole and complete is a result of integrating all the impressions, descriptions, dreams, feelings and reflections of one's self, past, present *and* future. I also began to see that these stories were a part of my personal, spiritual growth.

As I read and re-read *Everlasting Love,* I saw that this story was much more than a story about me or for me. I began to see that it is, truly, a story about life, for each and every one of us.

Rick and I spent entire nights, from bed time to the first quiet rays of sun light, talking about *Everlasting Love,* and how it was affecting us. The concept of traveling to and visiting other lives or incarnations was not entirely new to us. We had both taken part in many past life regressions. Regressions can feel very real, as though you are genuinely there in another time. But regressions had always had the feel of re-enactment and remembrance, seeing or being in something that has *already* occurred. We had certainly recognized the value of understanding better or discovering more in the events of the past.

My, and to a greater extent, Alara's traveling through time seemed to be much more like participating fully in the unfolding events and circumstances of another time. Alara seemed to be able to bring herself completely to another time, retain her identity, and affect reality as it was being created in that past time or as it is about to be created in a future time. It felt to us, as we discussed this process, that Alara, in her traveling, was bringing greater understanding to these other times and people, and bringing back greater wisdom and understanding to her own time.

In our discussions, we pondered the differences between the quality of Alara's time travels and our experiences with past life regressions. We were fairly sure that Alara did not have any magical abilities. But Alara certainly seemed to have more knowledge of the process of time travel and knowledge is power.

In one of those all night discussions we reminded ourselves that electricity and air travel were not invented but grew out of a greater understanding of natural forces. Electricity already existed; knowledge created the means for harnessing this power. Birds have flown for millions of years and as humans began to understand the properties of gravity, lift and aerodynamics, flight became possible by virtue of that knowledge. As people expand the envelope of belief, as we expand our ideas of what may be possible and dare to dream, what *is* possible also expands. In a sense, finding the means, or the *how*, of flight, electricity or time travel, is only detail.

After much discussion we realized that one of the most significant conditions of power is whether or not you know that you have it. We knew that each of us had at times felt powerless about one issue or another, only to discover that we were not powerless. I knew that in the past feelings of powerlessness had stopped me from taking action or moving forward.

When we applied these ideas to time travel, the conclusions were startling. Perhaps Alara believed or understood that time is malleable, not fixed. Perhaps she knew that past times are not finished and done but that, on their own level of existence, these past times are still alive and changeable. And allowing for these possibilities, perhaps Alara dared to sit down and talk with the past, only to find that the past responded. When Alara visited Frederick in his garden, her visit and the photograph that she brought changed Frederick and the future. When Rick and I had regressed into past lives, we had believed that the past was done, finished. Therefore, we never tried to affect the past, believing that to be impossible.

A door opened during those discussions by starlight and a shift began to take place somewhere in the cosmic machinery of the heavens or, in our viewpoint, of that machinery. Our eyes opened, too, and the possibilities were endless.

In our nightly discussions of *Everlasting Love,* we slowly began to realize that the theme of this story is simply and completely love. The story seemed to say to us that, in a loving universe, we are given the opportunity to live again and again. In this loving creation, we have the opportunity to exist eternally and to learn the fullness of love by working that vein of love. By resisting, misunderstanding, expressing and surrendering we become a purer more refined work of love.

Rick and I looked back at the lessons we had learned from past life regressions and added them to what we were learning from this story. The message seemed to be that, in this eternal theater of life, we meet each other over and over, cloaked in different guises, using new names, appearing in foreign lands. Each new drama presents us with a perfect new stage, a perfect set of circumstances, new tests, appropriate lessons, challenges and trials. We embrace, fear, loathe, become fascinated with these strange new people, though often times they are the same ones, here again, to work out that lesson of love.

On a beautiful full moon night, the room seemed to fill with a soft blue fog. We had talked into the quiet hours of pre-dawn. There was a tenderness between us that was becoming refined and strengthened as we shared the journeys of discovery launched by each new story. Our relationship, which we knew had blossomed in many lives together, was becoming deeper, closer. Rick said he could feel the stories and the story tellers channeling new energy into our lives, transforming us in the process.

During the month that it took me to complete this story, there occurred two other events that opened up to me new and exciting possibilities.

One night I had a very vivid dream about Maura and Danny. In this dream, much to my surprise, it was revealed to me that Maura and Danny, by different names, are friends of mine in this lifetime. Only a few months before starting this story, I had spent some time with them. In retrospect, I remembered wondering about the nature of their relationship. In my mind, I questioned some of the pain that seemed so much a part of their being together. On one level, it felt as though *Everlasting Love* was given to me, in part, as a response to my questions.

Everlasting Love helped me to see deeper into the dilemma that is a part of so many relationships. I could see that, as love purifies us, it bares in us those areas most in need of growth. In this struggle with love, our emptiness and fear are unearthed and pain is released. As we see and accept ourselves in this process, and understand and respect the other, we become more aware of our own wholeness.

As I looked at my friends, in the throws of their painful love, I felt that I shared some of Alara's hurt and frustration over Maura and Danny.

I was also fascinated by the thought that Alara might respond to pleas and questions in my heart and mind. I didn't realize, at the time, that this was just the beginning of a closer bond with that distant part of me, Alara.

A few days before finishing *Everlasting Love*, I sat down at my typewriter with a sense that this story was about to come to a close. The end of a story is always an event for me, a sometimes emotional and always a satisfying event. As the words began flowing through my mind and fingers on to paper, I realized that it was another story, a new story that was beginning to come through. I sat for a moment with the feelings that came up. A part of me longed for closure, the finishing of one journey before departing on another. I felt myself resisting this new beginning, needing the one to end before I could go on.

I found that I had to consciously and purposely let go of the unfinished story and my need for neat endings and beginnings. Since this incident, I have experienced this flow of events many times. I often have a number of works in progress, though something inside me secretly prefers to start and finish stories in sequence. When I look at time through Alara's eyes, it seems like we live many lives, in many different times, each life an unfinished work of art in progress.

A few nights later, I finished *Everlasting Love*. Within only a night or two, I completed *The Voice From The Bottom of The Sea*, which is the next story that I offer for your interest and enjoyment.

15

THE VOICE FROM
THE BOTTOM OF THE SEA

The door was open. David leaned partly against it but he was completely oblivious to the cool air trying to enter. Caught in a dreamland of his own, he sat alone at his table watching the wind blow a strange coldness down the streets of the island. David hunched over the table, motionless; his eyes gazed out through the window unseeing.

His position had barely changed for hours; no need to change. No one was in the cafe on this cool, windy evening. There was a stillness on the island and it was reflected in David's unmoving form. There was a great tension on the island also, a tension caught in the unusual cold breeze claiming the streets, adding a chill to the twilight sky. It was a cold sky tonight but not a heartless one. The chill in the air was a quiet one, and beautiful, unseen but felt by everyone.

David sat at the table, hour after hour, tapping a finger on his coffee cup. Tapping, tapping, tapping, the sound seemed to blend with the sound of the wind on the streets and the sound of the ocean outside the door. The cold clank of David's fingertip on the china cup seemed to become like the hands of a clock keeping perfect time. Everything seemed to blend and sound together, the breeze, the surf and David. Click, click, click ... everything moved to the same motionless beat. Tap, tap, tap ... David, the ocean, the wind and the sky were one. The island was tapping uneasily.

The tension felt heavy, resting in David's body, too heavy to move, too dense and alive to stay still. His left hand painfully clenched the cold cup and abruptly, his right finger stopped. For a moment he came out of his trance and with a quick burst, brought his lips to the cup and took a long sip. The cold coffee surprised his mouth and sent an icy chill through his teeth. The stone cold, bitter liquid poured quickly through his throat and sent a jolt of ice through his body, to deep within him. He shivered; the cold chill woke him up, out of his reverie.

He seemed to look around quietly and take in the room and then decide to go back, back to a warmer oblivion.

Even Millie the cook had gone home. David didn't like the aloneness of the cafe but he didn't like the aloneness of his oblivion either. He decided the cafe was better. He got up from his chair and stretched long and hard, trying to bring his body back, at least. He wasn't sure if his mind was ready yet.

"What's wrong with you David? You becomin' like the rest of 'em," Gelsey called, as she came through the swinging doors. "Put on some music, this place is like a tomb!"

"Good old Gelse (as David affectionately called her), her very presence is warming," David thought. She poured hot liquid into two cups and into the room. The steam drifted out and, for a moment, the world seemed a warmer place.

"David, perk up. Tomorrow night, you wait and see, this old place will be jumpin' with people, drinkin' and laughin'! I heard it's gonna be better tomorrow. The sun might even come out!"

"I couldn't run this place without you. You're always the optimist, Gelse! It's been a long time since we've seen the sun, hasn't it."

"Yeah," she said softly, the words dimming her light, "It's unnatural, it's unnatural all right, but it's not the end of the world. They's fools, is sayin that, that's all. You're not listenin to em, are you David? It just brings you all melancholy."

I had to smile as I sighed, "That's all you hear lately, but I'm not listening." It's funny, but I realized then, that it wasn't the unusual weather we were having that bothered me, or the lack of business, but that I was listening to another, even more painful voice.

Gelsey wanted to go on, "I know what's makin' you look so dark. It's that friend of yours that's comin', isn't it ... comin' for a visit."

"You always could read me, Gelse, more than anyone else," David sighed again.

"Old friends come back are like cold winds, sometimes," Gelsey said solemnly.

That's all we need, another cold wind around here, David thought. He could no longer sit still, he had to move. He got up and fled into the kitchen for some of the wise old lady's pie.

Diane sat at the table, stabbing quietly at her peach pie. She stared out at the window into a deep darkness, a darkness she knew, then, she had no understanding of, a darkness she knew, now, she feared.

"More coffee," the waitress said brightly?

"Sure, might as well," and Diane held out her cup, held it out and away from the darkness, lifted it to the light.

The waitress smilingly poured some of the hot, bright liquid into the cup and then fled through the busy room. The stuffy airport restaurant hummed with activity and noise but Diane heard only silence. She turned and faced the dark window again and wondered that she was so afraid. "Come on old girl, this isn't like you. In a few days, you'll look back and laugh at yourself." Still, it had been a long time. The thought called a tear into her right eye, a tear with a life of its own, separate from this woman of strength. But she allowed this coolness to fly down her cheek and fall silently into her coffee cup. She wiped her cheek uneasily and found her hand trembling.

"This is silly, this was a good idea! It's perfectly natural to see David while I'm here. He'll be glad to see me. It'll be different after all these years."

Still, all these delays bothered her. Was it the weather or an omen? After all, David had never answered her letter; maybe it never reached him. "Maybe he won't see me." And in that moment, she had the rush to fly back quickly, fly back and away from these dark, cold winds. "Why do I want to face them anyway?" The question pulsed in her head, over and over. She remained in her stiff seat though, silently staring at the dark clouds in the sky, unable to move, unable to admit her fascination with the cold sky.

She listened to one more announcement on the loud-speaker and knew she couldn't bear to sit here with this darkness for four more hours. She jumped to her feet, like an animal ready to lurch on its prey, and ran from the restaurant.

———

Overnight, the island seemed to have changed. Sunday night was entirely different. David moved through the glowing restaurant greeting customers, smiling, even seeming to laugh at times.

"Did you see the sun today!" It was on everyone's lips. Belief was in the stale cafe air.

Peter was working the bar with a smile on his face. "David, I'll tell you, Tommy and I were out in the yard and he said, 'Daddy! I know the sun will come out today, I know it!' And a few minutes later, there it was, brighter than it's ever been! I swear I even felt warm today!" David laughed.

"Where were you, David, did you see it?"

"Yeah Petey, I saw it, I was on the boat," David lied, as he walked away. Well, yes, he had seen it, all five minutes of it. He had been on his precious boat, the sweet Dee Marie. He had sat on the deck dreaming, thinking about Diane, looking up at the sun, and just when he realized that it really was the sun up there shining, it disappeared. He had thought it was a dream so, of course, he never really looked. He never did pick up his eyes and look at the warm sky.

David poured himself one more drink. Happiness filled the cafe. A peek at the sun had given people courage, had called them out of their homes and helped them shrug off the superstitions, the rumors of impending doom. He swallowed the strong, magical liquid quickly and felt the heat rush through his tired body. "Ahh," I felt it was worth it, coming to this lousy island for these drinks, alone. Then moments later, I was surprised to find that the fiery juice had burned some of the doom in my bones away, but still left just a trace of worry in my gut. Damn it, was there time for one more? But they were already pulling me, pulling me away. My friends and then everyone, pushing us up, me and Ben and Jon, pulling us to the middle of the room, laughingly.

I heard the sound of Jon's drums, and I couldn't wait to pick up the only other woman I loved, my fiddle. The night began.

Sometimes, on this beautiful dirt floor, my stage, jamming with Ben and Jon, I felt I was in heaven, no, I knew it. The world faded into nothingness, and we became the center, the sun. The light of the world flowed through us, flowed out from my fiddle, vibrated with the drums, sang in Ben's voice. Bodies danced with the heat from our light, and the noise and the music in the room became one song. The deck doors of the cafe were open tonight, and I could see a sparkling ocean dancing with the moonlight. I swear I felt the cafe's happy song join in with the singing island and the dancing ocean, and we became one voice. I was happy here, on this dirt floor, with my fiddle.

The night lingered on; amazing what one peek of the sun can do. The crowd danced on and on. It was a truly magical night. The moonlight in the room even looked like the sun; it looked golden. Tonight, no one wanted us to stop playing. We thought we could go on forever. I know I wanted to feel that fiddle in my hands forever, and tonight, forever seemed possible.

Ben's voice began singing an old island song. "If we live forever, if we live one day, doesn't ever matter, no one goes away."

The sea of drinking, dancing bodies, made the room hot. Everything seemed to slow up, the bodies began to move slower and slower, in a beautiful pattern, a beautiful haze of heat and life and motion. My fingers raced across my fiddle without thought from me. My brain slowed to match the room.

"Doesn't matter if you live one day. Spirits of the deep will come and take you away. If we live forever, we live today. Ocean spirit will call us someday. Ghosts in the water sing and dance here today."

Even the drums seemed to swirl and slow down. The room seemed to turn around, and then I saw the eyes of a spirit, dancing in the room, dancing with a body I knew. Something so familiar about the shoulders, the neck, her hair. The room danced and turned around again. Ben's smooth voice echoed and flowed on, "We used to live forever, but they called us away. Their voices called us away."

My eyes strained through the crowd, yearning for another glimpse of my familiar spirit. Then I saw her eyes dance, and peek through the crowd. So, my ghost from the past had arrived. Diane was here. My fiddle stopped playing.

The music went on without me. I crossed the room and took Diane's hands, and we danced. We moved to the heavy drum beat in silence, the three of us, Diane, my fiddle and me. It felt as if we could go on forever, or maybe we always had. But no, when Ben's voice came to a slow end, the crowd stopped moving. It was only us left in the middle of the room and I had to face the fact that we had stopped dancing, a long time ago. As the golden moonlight glowed through Diane's hair, I wondered to God why I had ever let go of her hands.

We sat at the table just staring at each other. I didn't want to talk, I knew what words had done to us in the past. But words have a funny way of insisting that they be said, and we began to talk.

"I am so glad to see you," and as I said it, I was amazed at how true the words were, truer than I'd ever thought they'd be. I was surprised at myself.

"Are you really ... you know I was afraid to come, it's been so long ... and you didn't answer my letter, I wasn't sure ..." It seemed hard for her to talk, too.

"I wanted to write, you know me. ...I didn't know what to say, I'm not much of a writer."

"You mean you won't write. You could have if you really wanted to," and then she caught herself, but too late. We both sat in the silence, remembering a very familiar feeling, a feeling of pain that couldn't or wouldn't change between us.

Diane finally broke the silence, "I'm very tired. Will we see each other tomorrow? Do you have time?" she asked uneasily.

"I have all the time in the world. I've saved all the rest of my moments for you." I tried to smile confidently. I felt like I wanted to cry. I wished I had said those words a long time ago.

———————

Diane couldn't sleep. She sat in the small room above the cafe, looking out the window, trying to make conversation with the moon for hours. She watched the sky turn from a calm, golden moonlight to a dark uneasiness, and the ocean begin to roar. She reviewed all the years of her life and her stormy time with David.

And here she was, she had come to this island for what? To finish off the storm with him? To quiet the fury raging inside of her? When she had arrived at the cafe last night and saw him standing in the crowd, playing his beloved fiddle, the storm had quieted down for a moment and her heart had cried with a joy she hadn't felt for a long time. His love for that precious violin had electrified the, crowd, as she'd seen so many times in the past.

She remembered back when David first got the fiddle. How he had felt every inch of it with his fingers, almost as if he was merging with it, taking it into his heart. She remembered how he had found a small carved hand symbol inside. They had wondered who had put it there and what it had stood for. They decided it was a symbol of their hands, joined as they always would be, Diane and David, going through life together, one hand.

They had joined hands then for a long time, maybe too long.

She said to herself, "When David first saw me tonight, I felt a wave of hope. When his eyes caught mine, I thought this time things might be different. When he came over and took my hands in his, I felt that's where they were meant to be and I would never let go. I remembered the time, long ago, when he had first taken my hands in his, and we began our life together. I remembered when David put his hat on the street and played that violin for all the strangers who passed by, and the few who listened and threw in a coin or two, coins that helped us eat, kept us alive. I cried as I realized I loved David's old fiddle as much as he did. I remembered how it had helped put me through school. I smiled at those days. It was hard to look back at those two people, strangers to me now. We were so happy. I was going to be a brilliant marine biologist and David was going to be the most famous musician the world had ever known. I think the world turned around once, while we weren't looking, and everything changed.

"Here I am, the unhappy biologist, miserable with her successful career and her life, and not knowing why, what happened. And David, who had he become? He had thrown the career he could have had, away, and here he sat on this island, far away from the world.

"When I came in and saw him playing, with that look of happiness on his face, I thought it was the same old David that I knew. I guess he still is, so irresistible, same old David smile, so sure of himself. When he said good-night, those words—'All the rest of my moments are for you.' How dare he say that to me again, after all this time. I remembered how I had lived for those words and for him, so long ago. How I had believed those words and David. How I had believed in that teasing smile. And even now, I knew we could have done it. We could have had our life together. We could have had everything. David could have been the star I wanted him to be. The three of us could have been happy, David, his fiddle and me.

"But he had thrown it all away. David had thrown me away, too, and here I was looking at his smile again and listening to the same words. What a fool! Why had I ever thought I was doing the right thing to come here. David would never change."

I threw things back in my just unpacked bag, I had made a mistake. I had a good, successful life to go back to, and I had to get out while I still could.

David tossed and turned furiously. His room at the back of the cafe was a very quiet room, but tonight was turning out to be a very noisy night. He listened to the sea roar, and get louder. Another storm was on its way.

"God, how long will this foul weather last!"

The fury of the waves crashing on the beach seemed to echo the crashing in my head. I realized that I didn't really care about the approaching storm though, there was a bigger storm already here, inside of me. It was that storm I was listening to, fighting with, raging against.

I was tired of fighting, fighting a ghost whose face I couldn't see. I thought I had escaped from that ghost, a long time ago. I guess I thought I had left it behind, and it would never find me on this island.

I've hidden for so long from her, I wondered if it was too late, too late to show myself. I wondered if I had the strength left. I wondered why now, after all these years, I even wanted to. I groped for the picture in the dark; I knew exactly where it was. The smooth, worn feeling of the photograph felt so right in my hands. I could see Diane's face in the darkness, without looking at it. I held it for a long time, and as the night turned into dawn, I knew what I would do.

I felt free. I watched the daily island plane take off in the distance, it looked beautiful in the stormy, pre-dawn sky. It filled me with a new sense of freedom. I went to sleep with a feeling of hope. At last, I could put my head down and rest.

When I awakened, I felt as if I'd slept for a year, even though the clock told me it had only been an hour. I felt refreshed, better than I'd felt in years. I looked out of my window and was surprised to find that, even though the storm inside of me had died, the cold winds outside were still building. "Oh well," I thought, "the smell of Millie's home-cooked breakfast will warm up the cafe." As a cold shiver ran up my spine, I knew I was sick of the cold winds. It was time, at last, to warm up my life.

———

Up in the air, Diane was sick. The tossing of the sky matched her emotions. She stared out of the plane at the dark heavens, and felt the only real sense of doom she had ever felt in her life. Everything was weighed, over and over, "Maybe I should have told him I was going. Would he have stopped me?" And with those thoughts, she had a feeling, and knew then it was too late to stop. The winds that were coming, had finally arrived.

———

When Gelsey told him she was gone, he was shocked, he didn't believe her, wouldn't believe her. He raced to the empty room, and sat on the bed looking like he'd just seen a ghost. Then slowly, as he thought of Diane, thought of her flying out of his world, his face changed, and a new and permanent silence filled the cafe.

Gelsey paced in the kitchen, while Millie prayed.

"I knew it, I felt it in my bones I did. I tried to tell him about that girl comin here ... and then I thought, seein' 'em together last night, it might be all right, maybe I was wrong. I shoulda known then, I ain't never wrong when I feel it in my bones. And now he's actin' like a crazy man, out there in that boat in this weather! He'll catch his death ..."

Millie cried, "it's the end, it is, it's comin, we never had no winds like this before! And Sal said so. God be with us! God be with us!"

"Oh shut up, Sal's just an old witch. The Gods of this island can fight any Gods of the sea," Gelsey said uneasily, as she watched the ocean roar.

David sat on the Dee Marie crying, completely oblivious to the waves crashing over the deck. He picked up his beloved fiddle, clung to it tightly for a long moment, and then closed his eyes and began to play. He played his heart out for the raging sky and he played his life out for the Gods of the sea. No music was ever heard before like it, or ever will be heard again.

David's sound blended with the crashing drums of the sky and the intense sound of the waves, and their music became one.

———

On Diane's flight back everyone, even the pilot, was terrified.

I felt numb; I knew I was flying to my death and I didn't care. I knew I had to come back. The few passengers on the small plane prayed and screamed on our turbulent ride through hell, and no one could believe that when we landed, I had refused to get off the plane and flown back to the island. Fate? I flew back to be with my God and David.

It was a miracle that we were able to land. When I found what was left of the cafe I had to stop myself from panicking anew. A dying Gelse told me David had gone out on the boat, and I knew I had to try and find him. I knew chances were worse than none but I fought, fought to find him, fought to stay alive while the world around me died.

I grabbed David's scuba gear and went out on the skiff. There was no sign of the Dee Marie. I started diving and still couldn't find a trace. The equipment became heavy on my back. I ached to throw it off and give up. The ocean called me, "Diane, let go," but I still kept fighting.

One last dive and I knew he had gone, left me forever. Then I saw it, at the bottom of the sea, the most beautiful fiddle that had ever sung. With one last great effort, I brought it up to my boat and sat and held it close to me. I felt for the indentation, the mark inside, and as I felt my finger on our *hand*, my boat gave up and I went to join the sea.

I watched as the storm completely swallowed up the island and the Gods swallowed up my world.

I floated down for an eternity. Instead of becoming heavy, my body began to feel lighter as I made my descent through the door of the ocean. There was no more struggle, no more fight. I let go and listened to the music of some distant angel.

It was a relief. I wrapped myself around the fiddle tightly and we drifted downward together, oh so slowly. We flew through the water together, it was like dancing. And as my darkness turned to light, I heard David singing to me.

I gave up and floated down to a voice from the bottom of the sea.

16

FACING THE STORM

As I finished typing the last few lines of *The Voice From The Bottom of The Sea,* I could feel inside myself a tremendous flow of emotional release and surrender. I felt as if I had just returned from my own final moments, from my own dreamy descent towards the ocean floor. It took me a few minutes to realize who and where I was and that I was still very much alive. I had become that involved in the story.

I had watched closely as David and Diane's story slowly unfolded. I had felt a storm gathering, a building whirlwind of colliding forces, the ebb of fear and uncertainty and the flow of love and yearning. I found myself pulling for them, hoping that they would see the depth of their shared love, hoping that they would admit it, stop fearing and denying it.

At the same time, I could feel the cold chill of past currents that had run through my own life. I knew that, in my own life, love and trust had not been easily embraced. I could feel the storms of love that I had survived, the risks of being vulnerable that I had taken. These were some of the most compelling challenges that I had ever encountered.

The story passed through me like a wind, rustling my senses, stirring up my emotions. As David and Diane gave voice to their feelings, I could feel them touch me as if they were my own. I sensed their longing for warmth and oneness. I felt their dreams grown cold and empty without the other. I remembered, as if it were part of my own memory, the sparks of clashing differences that were part of their past together. I was fascinated, mesmerized, by the cold darkness that had descended in its place.

I looked back at my life and my experiences of love. I knew that love, whether of family, friends or partners and marriage, always challenged my sense of identity. The fear of losing boundaries or identity in relationship to another has always been present for me. And yet, I have always found that love expands my identity, opening me to new visions, strengths and qualities. I wished that David and Diane would see this, even as the storm clouds gathered.

In the end, after much conflict, they each faced the storm and the darkness. They came to recognize their own resistance. It's as if resistance is an island in a sea of surrender. The physical island and their islands of resistance dissolved and surrendered to that totality, love.

Initially, I felt sad, as if they had finally surrendered, but too late. At the same moment, I remembered Maura and Danny and their many lives together. Somehow it all came together for me in that moment, the realization that their surrender wasn't too late, that the opportunity for oneness and love exists forever in each moment. In their surrendering to love, David and Diane expanded their own identities beyond fear and ego. And in a loving universe, death is only the opportunity to begin again

The next story, *Darkness Into Light,* is also about those moments of beginning and renewal, and the shamans that tend the flame that turns darkness into light.

17

DARKNESS INTO LIGHT

Looking up from the street, my window could only be seen from a certain angle. The old building had so many walls and corners that seemed to jut out in different directions. It always seemed to be hiding some of itself away from the world, concealing some of its angles, some of its windows, some of its life.

The aging edifice had been home to so many, through the long years, and all five stories were filled with a quiet energy and the dust left from many lives. It was an imposing structure but graceful with a calmness that comes to the very old. The way it stuck out onto the sidewalk in different places always made me feel that it somehow wanted to give some of its grace and quiet to the passing world. It imposed its past onto the street for all the world to see but no one ever noticed. I don't think anyone ever does notice the way the past just naturally projects itself into the present, or do we? Sometimes we do see a kind shadow or a cruel dream pass by in the background, in corners, behind curtains.

So many things were hidden by this beautiful building. From every side it created a different point of view. Sometimes it seemed like a fortress, to protect, or a welcoming shelter, or to divide, as the world always asks for divisions. Sometimes it enclosed secrets, like my window, which could only really be noticed from one spot on the sidewalk, and only if you were standing still and looking up. No one ever stood still.

Every day, late in the afternoon, I gave some time to my window. I would sit in my worn velvet chair and relax and watch. I enjoyed this time. My body would sink deeper and deeper into the golden, velvet, overstuffed chair and I would feel a great peacefulness come over me. I loved the way the puffy, yellow pillows felt and how they seemed to reach up and absorb my tired body. They seemed to cushion my tired soul and hold me in a safe place in which to watch the world outside. And that was what I came to this chair for, my daily ritual of quietly, thoughtfully, waiting and watching my world. My position was perfect. I would ease the pillows towards the window, slowly easing towards the world.

My precious opening to the world was framed in mahogany, a color that would always cast a warm, satiny glow on the world inside my window. The large, shiny pane of glass faced out from a strangely shaped corner on the third floor of the building that had grown into my home. I had three rooms but only one window and I treasured it. Every day it seemed to give me a new view of the world. It faced out on a busy street, busy with the life and blood of many spirits who moved and pulsed in their windowless world. I loved to watch it all, to open my window and my being, and take it all in.

The twilight was my favorite time of day. I relished every moment as the light dimmed and spread out through the glittering sky. It seemed to cast gold sparkles on the street and its faces. I waited and watched as the sun gracefully and slowly danced away from view and spread its fire out, flying through the sky so givingly, suffusing the world with light, one last gift to the world. It always gave me a funny feeling. I felt compelled to watch. I had to watch, just in case it never happened again. It became a ritual. The sun's daily ritual became mine.

On this particular Tuesday, the early evening was alive with color. The sky had turned from a reddish gold to a lush, velvety, cool violet. The color was like a haze, a thick cloud of violet, hanging over the night, waiting.

I sat for a long time on my golden throne of comfort, elbows on the sooty window sill, feeling like a queen, privileged to view her kingdom clothed in a dazzlingly, royal light. My window always seemed higher than it really was because of the angle of the building, but tonight it felt even higher. I felt as if I was on top of a cloud of violet, hovering over the city of lights.

I watched every moment as the purple sky descended to darkness. As the lights of the city came on, it was startlingly beautiful. I couldn't bear to move from my window seat. I wanted to watch every new moment of my world, glittering and changing colors. It was like a kaleidoscope of people and lights and darkness. The people on the street below me were like little jewels, hurrying through the blackness of night, bits of colored glass, forming symmetrical patterns by reflecting themselves as the world quietly rotated.

I watched them come and go, laden with packages, dogs, children and each other. I always wondered that so few held hands, so few smiled. They seemed so busy, carrying the world on their backs, too burdened with the weight to notice the ribbon on their packages, too oppressed with heaviness to stop for even a moment and open their gifts. Their eyes were always on the ground; for them there was no sky.

The streetlight on the corner was one of the last to turn on. I was just about to leave my cozy seat of illumination, but I stopped, attracted by a dark figure standing motionless under the light. A coldness seemed to emanate from him. There was a terrible aloneness in his face. His eyes looked wet. I'm not sure if was tears or ice that I saw there. The only thing I understood was the incredible energy coming from his heart. I knew him well. My heart understood his energy, his aloneness. I felt afraid for him, standing alone with the light and the darkness, unable to reach out to either one. I watched his struggle from my window. I waited as he moved slowly down the street, out of step with the world. He moved to a distant sound, a noise that scared him deeply. He seemed to walk in time with a beat that was keeping him alive but ever so slowly driving him over the edge. As he passed by and went on into the night,

I listened to the music of his being. I wondered when we would meet.

—————

Jason walked slowly down the street, feeling alone with the darkness of a cold city. It was his favorite time, this period from sunset to darkness. He liked to be watching when the night descended on his city, the city of lights.

It's such a gradual decline, he thought, the death of the sun each day. He smiled to himself; he knew all about gradual declines. He knew them too well. He enjoyed his feeling of aloneness, too. It had become part of him. He always felt alone, even though there were many people bustling around him, hurrying home from their day's work.

It was cold but he didn't care. He was used to the cold, it was the way of the city, an imposing facade, he felt concealing something else, he didn't know what. For a brief moment, he went back, remembering the small town where he was born and had spent his first twelve years. He had always felt warm there. It had been so nice to feel warm. Then he allowed himself to feel the raw dampness, for one moment, and he wondered if he'd ever know warmth again.

It was starting to get dark; the lights of the city were blinking on. As a street light over his head went on, Jason stopped, hesitated, and looked up at the light. He wondered when he had allowed the coldness of this city to enter him. Had he given his permission? He didn't even remember a fight. For a moment he was sorry, infinitely sorry; he wondered if it could have been different. Then he shrugged off the chill and continued on into the darkness.

The pilgrimage through the city lasted for hours. Jason walked and walked, turning over his life with each step. The trip was punctuated by visits to a few of his regular haunts. By the time he reached his last stop, his favorite, he was feeling much better. He always wondered why he liked this dingy bar so much, it was old, dirty, dark. Yeah, it's the darkness, he thought. It was so completely black, he always had the feeling he could get lost in its darkness, melt completely in this velvety bar and disappear. He liked the feeling but he wasn't sure why. It was always a familiar feeling. He felt at home here. He felt close to everyone who worked here, especially Rico the bartender. He could see himself in most of the faces of the customers and he was especially close to Sandy, a regular of this holy shrine. They were his family, Rico and Sandy, they and the band were his only friends, his only family.

Tonight though, he wanted no part of family or friends. He only wanted to be alone with his head. He thought he was home free, Rico was busy listening to the problems of another customer. Then Sandy walked in, intruding too abruptly into his building forgetfulness.

"God, I don't have to ask how the audition went. I can see it all over you!" Sandy sat down with too much noise.

"Well good, if you can see it, we don't have to talk about it," Jason snapped.

"Oh Jesus, you're not gonna run that game again, are you? You know it helps to talk about it, gets you through all those feelings of rejection."

"I don't have any feeling of rejection."

"Oh sure, I can tell. You're fast on your way to feeling nothing. Why didn't they like the band anyway?"

"They just ... didn't ... like ... us. Said we weren't right. Our sound wasn't right."

"Ah, the magic word, right. I'm sick of that one myself. How're the other guys taking it?"

"Phil's taking it fine, as always. Says, why should we get uptight, just because they don't recognize talent, it's their loss. Michael and Steve are getting kind of down though ... I don't know."

"Yeah, I know how it is, I really do, it's the same scene for me." And Sandy put her hand in mine. It felt warm.

"What are you guys gonna do now? What's the next step?" Sandy tugged at her jingling earrings.

"I don't know, I'm not sure if there is a next step. I'm really sick of next steps."

"Come on now, that's not Jason talking ... that's the bottle on the table crying."

"I'm tired of talking, Sandy. I'm tired of everything. I'm tired of this whole stinkin' city. I'm so tired."

"God Jason, I don't like the way you sound. You can't take it like this. I've heard you play. You're damn good and I'm not saying that cause I'm your friend."

"Yeah, sure, I've got talent ... ha, ha ..."

"I know what you need. I just found this incredible lady. She lives in the village and I've got a session with her next Monday. You can come with me."

"That's all I need. What are you seeing, two analysts now, Sandy?"

"No, Helen's my analyst, and I see her on Wednesdays, which wouldn't be so bad for you either. But Rosie's different, she does magic, she can tell you what to do with your life. She knows how to summon up the spirits, she knows everything. I went to see her last week and she was incredible!"

"Oh God, that's all I need, some Voodoo lady. I might as well hang it all up now. You're a sucker Sandy, you know that."

"I am not ... but have it your way. That's what you get when you try to turn a friend on to a good thing, insults! I know your future anyway, you don't need Rosie ... you're gonna sit here for the rest of your life and let that bottle turn you on. Enjoy yourself Jason. Sit here in the darkness ... I'm going."

As she left, Jason breathed a sigh of relief and slowly slid back into the shadows.

———•—•———

Jason didn't want to go to the practice session but he found himself there anyway. He stopped before he opened the door, stood in the narrow hall, and listened. He listened to a roomful of music, a world full of joyous sound. He wanted to cry, they sounded that good, the three of them. They were damn good, even without him. Did he really add anything to the music, he wondered? The song was beautiful, though. It still made him cry to hear it. That same old feeling still welled up from his toes to his head, just like on the day he wrote it.

He leaned up against the dirty, obscene wall with its chipping green paint and he got lost in their music. There is a heaven on Earth, he thought, and who would have guessed it, its here in this filthy hallway.

His mind flew away, listening to the sound. Listening to the words, "losing the one I need," made him remember everything he'd ever lost in his life. From the dad who died to the pretty girl who'd walked out on him to the Jason he used to be. He cried like a man who'd lost the last thread of his life.

And where had it gone? Was it back at the old house in Tennessee? How had he lost it? It had disappeared ever so slowly, when he wasn't looking, when he couldn't see, when he was too busy fighting, struggling, wondering, trying to make some sense of his world.

When had it all fallen away? Somehow it had gotten lost in his day to day existence. Disappeared into the dust that was left when he tried to find the real Jason and tried to make that pure, unadulterated version, into something.

The dust had turned into a white dust and it had become his friend, helped him. Helped him to build up a strong immunity to the world. Helped him with the struggle the world had become for him. The soothing white dust and his golden bottle had given him part of his skin. That beautiful powder had given him the armor with which to face his world. It was crumbling now, though, and he didn't understand why. The thickness of his skin was gone and he wondered how long he could live without it.

He listened to his band make their music, pound their drums. He listened in the quiet, dark hall and then he left. He knew he couldn't sing his songs anymore. The drums in his heart had died.

He found himself hiding in his refuge of darkness again, faced with the saving bottle again. It had become a sacred place for him. The only thing missing was Sandy.

His sanctuary needed a priestess. Where was she? She was always here on Monday nights and he wanted her here now. Her approval was all he needed to make him free from all his sins. And where was she? He developed an overpowering need for her to be there.

Then he remembered. This was the night she went to see her witch. Aah, the thought tickled him. She was the one who needed saving, not him. He thought about it for a while and then he decided he was up for it, he could do it. He would save Sandy from her Voodoo shrink. He was equal to the task. He set out through the door and into the darkness of the street.

Rico had known where to find Sandy's witch, thank God, or all would have been lost. He would have failed in his virtuous quest. But the fates were with him, he could still save Sandy, if he hurried.

Jason found himself in a part of the village he didn't know very well. All at once, the dark, old buildings seemed imposing. They seemed like fortresses, protecting some evil spirits, forbidding him to enter or even look into their windows. The cold of the streets seemed to snap at him, sobering his soul. What was he doing here? What a fool! Well, he did want to see Sandy. He thought of her warm, familiar smile.

He found the number he was looking for on a large, decrepit, old brownstone but he hesitated. What was he doing here? He thought of walking Sandy home, the talk they would have, what she would say, how she would scold him, how she would understand. He rang the bell of the apartment on the third floor.

As he walked up the stairs, the silence in the hall began to enter his being. He began to remember who Jason pretended to be, his sanity and his manners. When he arrived at the door, he straightened his winter jacket and his moth-eaten scarf and he thought, "I look like Jason, now, I'm ready." He knocked on the door, stepped back into the safety of the hallway and took a deep breath of stale air. It was the last breath he took for a number of long moments.

She was small and beautiful and unimposing. How strange, he thought. When she asked him to come in, he found himself entering her tiny apartment, even though he could hear the words that she was saying clearly enough. Sandy was not here, she had called to change her time, she had an audition ... needed time to rehearse ... a new dance ensemble forming ... she was so excited.

And then she smiled, Rosie did, and she laughed, and the sound lit up the room, the world and Jason's heart.

"You're not afraid of me, are you? Sandy told me a little about you, said she had a friend who should come to see me. She wasn't at all sure if she could convince you."

"I'm not afraid," *I lied*, "you just look different. You're so young, pretty ... I don't see any crystal balls. I don't know."

"Aah, but I do have a crystal ball. Do you want to see it?"

"No, I mean ... you ... you don't look like a witch ..."

"I'm not a witch. I'm a dancer, like Sandy. Well ... at least I used to be, before the accident. Now, I'm a shaman, at least I practice the shamanic arts. It's not witchcraft. I'm a healer. I like to think of myself as a medicine woman ... and I see visions, sometimes, things that seem to help people ... never bad things."

"I ... I don't know, you look normal enough." I tried to smile.

"I like you, Jason, so I'm not going to take that as an insult," and she threw back her head and laughed ... such a beautiful laugh.

"Besides, I know you Jason. I saw you once in a vision, right over here."

She took my hand, and led me over to a big, gold chair.

"Come over here, sit down, and look out of my window, Jason. I'm so glad you found me."

Rosie seemed so easy to talk to, nothing like I thought a witch would be ... I mean a shaman. I sat on a chair by her window and I found I wanted to stay. There was something so familiar about her, so friendly. I began to relax and even enjoy myself.

She made some tea for us ... awful looking stuff, dark and strange, but surprisingly, it tasted good. I began to feel more like myself and almost happy.

Rosie told me about her life, about the years she'd trained as a dancer. How heart broken she'd been after the accident. How she had always seen "pictures," seemed to know, even as a child, what was going to happen. How she had been introduced to the way of the shaman.

I told her about my life and even the things I didn't tell her, she seemed to know, seemed to see them in my eyes. I felt naked in her presence, sitting by Rosie's window. It felt good. It felt as if all the aloneness of my life was stripped away. Someone knew. Someone saw. Rosie seemed to see inside me and it felt like a relief, a breath of fresh air to be seen. No one had ever really seen me before, not even me.

We talked for a long time over the sweet smelling, muddy tea. Her white candles scented the air and made me drowsy, as if I were floating in a garden where time stood still and everything stopped and waited for Rosie's laughter.

"You know you are one of us Jason, a shaman. You are in touch with the pulse of the Earth. Sometimes it scares you, it beats so loudly in your heart. Sometimes you try to stop it and you panic when you can't. And sometimes you are one with it and you create a sound, a sound so beautiful that even the people of the Earth can hear it."

Her words startled me and scared me. "No Rosie, I'm a talentless musician who truly loves music. But I've always been luckless, directionless, only one small sound, somewhere in the wind. I'm a loser, Rosie, one of the city's creatures of no consequence. The wind takes me wherever it wants and it leaves me there alone."

"Jason, the wind's sound is one of the most beautiful sounds that ever was created. You are a sound of that wind, Jason, and a most beautiful one. You say you truly love music, that love is a gift, an ability that you've carried with you for a long, long time. Listen to it Jason, hear it, listen to it so closely that you become one with it. It will give you power, the power you need to do what you came here to do. It will guide you Jason. It will give you the music you need to live."

I thought of Rosie, as I walked home that night. And I thought of her in the many days that followed, strange days, uneasy days. I felt different after that night but I wasn't sure why. I knew I had lived too long with trouble, only some unheard beat of the world had kept me going. And I began to listen to that fading beat.

I wasn't sure, what exactly, was different. Nothing looked like it had changed. I asked Steve and Michael if I looked different, if I sounded different, and they laughed. The air did seem different though, but I didn't know how to breathe this new air. I wondered if it was Rosie who had brought this new breeze into my life. I didn't know why I longed to see her again but I wanted to know. I wanted to learn to breathe again.

When I called her, I felt like a fool. I heard her giggle on the other end of the line.

"You want me to show you how to breathe again Jason, how to listen to that strange beat of your heart? Yes, of course I can, that's what us medicine women are for!"

I could see her eyes laughing through the telephone wire. I couldn't wait until eight o'clock.

The sound of my knock on her door seemed to echo through the old walls forever before she came to the door, limping. She smiled as she caught me looking down at her foot. I don't know what it was but there seemed to be something so powerful about her. There was such a contrast to her presence, her injured leg did not fit at all. It was the first time I noticed it, when she came to the door that day, and also the last.

She led me into an empty room, bare except for white candles and scented air. "This is where I do my meditations, Jason. Every day at sunrise and sunset I am here. This is my medicine room, I am a shaman here, this is where I do my work."

"Is this going to hurt, lady?" I tried to smile as I tugged at my scarf.

"Yes, Jason, it's going to hurt. It's going to hurt more than anything's ever hurt before. It will hurt so much, you'll pray for anything to take it away. The pain will become so intense, so real, in every bone and muscle and nerve. It will feel as if your body is being torn apart, leaving your mind to drift through some listless hell, alone. Kind of like dying, Jason." She smiled as she put my hands in hers. They felt warm.

She put some music on and it sounded pretty, too pretty, like flutes in some springtime meadow. I began to feel more frightened than I've ever felt in my life. She poured me some of her dark, pretty tea and I put it up to my lips but I was afraid to drink. She looked at me sharply, a little too sharply.

"Relax, Jason, it will all be over before you know it," and she stopped and smiled, a little too sadly.

"Now that's just what I'm afraid of." My turn to smile.

"Are you afraid, Jason?" And she looked at me in such a way that I knew my lying days were over.

"Yeah, I'm more than afraid, but I guess I've always been that way. I don't know why. I don't know of what. Maybe I'm afraid of the darkness, maybe the light, maybe the world. Maybe you. Yes, you."

"Do you want to know what you're afraid of, Jason. Do you care?"

"No I don't care ... I don't care anymore." And I drank her bittersweet tea.

"Have you lost every shred of hope, is there nothing left?" She looked so sad.

"No, God, there is nothing left for me."

"Are you very sure?" She asked slowly.

I nodded. I couldn't speak anymore.

"Jason, look at me. Tonight you are ready, ready to come into this room. At some point, you will want to know what it is, what you are afraid of. And I want you to remember when that moment comes, your courage will come with it."

I thought she was going to put her arms around me then, I think she wanted to. Instead she embraced me with her eyes. It was a long, long embrace.

"Jason," she said, "It's time." Her smile was gone. Her face was touched with a deep seriousness, from some other place. "Come dance with me, Jason," and she pulled me to my feet.

The music seemed to change, it seemed to become louder, more powerful. The flutes became trumpets, heralding some arrival. The sounds seemed to deepen and become more alive. Yes, the room was alive all right. Every corner seemed to make its own noise. Even the floor seemed to jingle with new life as it met Rosie's bare toes.

I knew it was time too. Yes, I could turn back, it was in my hands. I could turn back and refuse to play.

"Come dance with me," every wall, every corner of the room seemed to call me. The beckoning sounds seemed to call me through the thick, scented air. It was time to answer.

The tension in the room created soft waves, motions of energy to float on, hide in, tremble with. The thick, strange music echoed everywhere. Rosie stood on the other side of the room and closed her eyes. She began to change, her face seemed to slowly transform itself. I felt like she was far away. She seemed to be calling someone or something but I couldn't hear her words.

I gave out one last prayer, a childish verse I remembered from my days in Tennessee. I closed my eyes and I began to dance and as the music took its hold on the room, I knew I was going to die.

The wild pounding of my heart seemed to match the drums of the music, and I couldn't tell, after a while, which one it was that was rushing through my ears. All at once, a great wind blew through the room. It seemed to whip up the air into a frenzy. The walls and the floor seemed to shake with rage. The ceiling disappeared. The very air seemed to be battling with itself. The light became dim, truly, we were in darkness. The candles were losing their struggle to burn on, in this terrible wind. The room was thick with clouds of smoky energy. I lost all sight of Rosie. I was afraid! I felt unarmed, alone, unable to breathe in this conflict. The drums of the music became louder and louder, until they pounded all through my head, forcing their angry sound into my veins. The drums began their battle with the wind.

The dazzlingly steady beat seemed to be summoning me, and my body began to shake violently in response. The medicine room became alive with a hellish beat. My body began to die with pain. The world circled around and around, rocking with anguish.

I began to hear screams piercing the darkness, hushing the little light remaining. I found my hands on the pulsing floor, it was hot, sticky. The music became intensely loud and began to fight with the screams, coming from all directions. The damnable sounds fought with the wild drums and a tremendous noise came shuddering through the air and entered my head. The noise became a beat that went all through my body, cutting sharply through the thick, cold pavement of my heart. The beat went straight through the floor, throbbing into the deep bowels of the old, dark building, down into the black ground, below the earth.

My body danced with uncontrollable spasms that shook my being. It felt as if one sharp claw formed out of the music and reached in, deep inside me, to rip open my heart. I felt like I was leaving my body, slowly. I heard Rosie moan, "Let him live ... awaken him ... give him life!"

I died.

When I opened my eyes, it was to a new light. I felt weak, trembling. I struggled to move my limbs, like a newborn baby. The first thing I saw was Rosie, there in front of my eyes, filling them with her life.

She was still dancing like a dream. An angel of the air, moving with the wind, dancing with the sound. I raised myself up a little to watch her. I have never before in my life seen anyone dance like Rosie did on that night, and I know I will never see anyone dance that way again.

I thought I must have hallucinated myself into some strange world where nothing physical existed. There was only air, energy and magnificent light. A golden haze seemed to fill the room. There were no walls, no ceiling, no floor. Only a vast, sparkling energy moved and breathed and floated out into the world, a world with which we could dance.

And Rosie danced with it all, took hands with the light, with the gods of the air and the spirits of the world, flew with the brilliant energy surrounding her. Rosie did not dance with the music; instead, the music danced with her. It enfolded her and lifted her up. It embraced her and caressed her very being, lovingly holding her feet, affectionately becoming a part of her. She seemed to fly with sound.

My eyes felt as if they never wanted to move again. I was transfixed. Then she came to me and took my hands, gently lifting me to my feet, and we floated through the air. We danced with a beautiful sound, a sound I'd never heard before. I felt free, light, lost in the magical, crystalline force surrounding us. We danced for a long, long time, moving with the fire and the passion of the music, the most beautiful music I had ever heard. I felt one with a light that I had never seen before.

The drums of the music slowly became the drums of my heart. The room was filled with a quiet thunder that compelled us to move, entered our beings and kept us going. Rosie moved in perfect time with some melodic beat of the universe. I have never before seen anyone who had such perfect timing. I've never known a time so perfect.

We flew with the bright, white energy in the room for hours and we looked out of Rosie's window. I saw a flash of lighting come across the sky, through Rosie's glass, and enter my heart, leaving there a strength that felt warm. We danced together until the darkness turned to light while the sun slowly came up in a violet sky.

When I left the recording studio, I felt happy, happy with the knowledge that Steve and Phil, Michael and I would be pounding our drums together for a long time. And who would have thought it, after all these years, people were paying us to do it. They couldn't seem to pay us enough. I laughed deeply at the thought. I breathed very easily these days.

Still, I knew when I had put my signature on that golden piece of paper, a few months ago, that I was closing some doors. The band and I would be walking down some very different hallways.

Tonight we would fly out, first stop on our first world tour. I walked slowly, enjoying my city, savoring the lights I would not see for a long time. I knew I should be going home, packing up the final touches, but I couldn't go yet. I had to see her once more.

She met me at the door, looking very unsurprised, laughing her beautiful sounds. "Jason, what a surprise!" I took her hands and they felt so warm, I wasn't sure if I could ever let go.

"You know we're leaving tonight, first concert on the tour coming up!"

"You must be so excited. You're going to love it, Jason, I can see it in your eyes. It will be an incredible success, the first of many."

"Well, I thought you might have changed your mind, Rosie … you might come with me. You'd enjoy it, we'd have a great time, and we'd be together."

She smiled as she let go of my hand. "I can't, Jason, there's somewhere else for me."

"Where, here? You can't stay here … you could be dancing, dancing on stage. You should have everything, Rosie … you deserve everything. I have the money now. We can find the best doctors in the world, the best therapy."

"No, Jason, all the money in the world can't buy me another leg. There's nothing more that can be done. But it doesn't matter, it took me a long time to realize it, but I know, now, what I came here to do," she said softly, sadly.

"I didn't come here to dance for the world, only for some very special people."

"Come with me, Rosie, I know what you are ... I know about your miracles, more than anyone. I'd never try to change you. I love you ... I love what you are. The world needs more shamans and I need you, Rosie. Come with me, we'll heal the world together."

"It's a wonderful thought, Jason. The world will be lucky to have you. Your sounds will be heard in many different ways and will heal for a long, long time to come. You know what to do ... you don't need me ... you know where you are needed. People will find you when they need you and you will know them, Jason. There are always shamans. They come in many sizes, shapes and colors. They look different, they sound different, and if you need one, the right one will always find you. You may not recognize him, but he will find you. Shamans learn to know where their place is."

"I'll always dance, you know that, Jason, just as you will. Our dance is our life, our way. The beat will always be there for us to hear. You will always know what to do, if you listen to it."

"But I don't want to go through this life without you. I love you, Rosie."

"I love you too, Jason, but there is somewhere else for us now. But ... don't you know it ... you'll never be without me. Feel my heartbeat, Jason," and she put my hand on her chest. "We will always be together. We will always hear the same beat, wherever we go in this world. You know what to do, Jason ... you don't need me anymore. You have so many things to do, so many places to go, so much music to play, so many to heal. Go on your way, Jason. You'll always take me with you and I'll always take you." She laughed through shiny eyes as she forced me through the door, pushed me into the first hallway of the rest of my life.

There was much music in my life, through the years. Golden concerts, golden records, golden people filled all my days. The only thing I ever missed was some silence, once in a while, and Rosie. I thought of her often; she had somehow become a part of me. I heard her words often, her laughter sometimes, in the night. Her way had grown into my way. I was always conscious of the path of healing. Though I sometimes wondered what kind of shaman I had become.

It wasn't always an easy way. Not when producers, agents, investors and even the public, wanted you to be something else. I struggled, through the years, with many demons of the world. Greed, insecurity, power, it always amazed me how, if I managed to close the door on one, down the road a little, another would show its face. I won the battle sometimes, and I lost sometimes, but I never gave up trying.

And I never stopped listening; I never stopped hearing that beautiful heartbeat of the world. I always thought that I was most in touch with it during concerts. I would step out there on that heavenly platform and look at the crowd and feel a great surge of power go all through me.

I especially looked forward to tonight's concert. It felt like we had played a thousand nights, this year, but I still looked forward to stepping out there in front of the crowd. Performing still filled me with an excitement that I'd only known on one other night of my life. Tonight's date was the last one for a long time. At last we all had a lengthy vacation to enjoy. It had been a very long year. It was an outdoor concert and those were my favorite. I liked to stand on that stage and look up at the sky. The glaring stage lights made it hard to see but once in a very great while, I'd catch a glimpse of a small, bright star.

Tonight was a warm, beautiful night. There was a velvety softness resting on the world. The four of us were filled with the relief of a tour almost over and the crazy expectancy of one more night. One more time to give it all we had, and we were ready. We were ready to walk out on that stage, feeling strong and happy, anxious to get the job done, and filled with a thirst to enjoy this last night to the fullest.

I took one last deep breath, as I always did backstage, and it was time to face the lights. I strutted out on stage to the noise of the swollen, vibrating crowd. Thousands of bodies, dancing to our music, flashing their lights in the night. A more incredible sight you could never find. It always left me more than a little breathless. It always took the wind right out of my lungs and made my throat choke for a few minutes.

Thousands of expectant little spirits that could no longer control the great energy they had created for the occasion, they filled the arena with a great sound until it was ready to explode, as it always did, a great burst of noise, filling the arena and flying outside through the world.

It was the same, wherever we went, whatever small town or big city, in every part of the world. A mass of beings waiting to be entertained, taken care of, maybe even saved. I would put my hands out to the throng and listen until I could hear that same familiar beat, feel it pulsing through my veins, and then I would try to give them what they wanted, and something that they needed.

But this night was different. I knew it the moment I stepped out on the stage. There was a strange feeling in the air and I felt distracted. I tried to close myself off from an unusual feeling that fate was waiting for me in the wings. Final night jitters ...? Maybe.

I gave myself to the music and the crowd. It was kind of like a sacrifice, I always thought. I offered myself to the gods of sound, my silent prayers, as the crowd screamed. Then I would begin to feel the noise of some far away drums, mingle with the ones on the stage, and start to vibrate through me.

Tonight, though, it seemed as if an even stronger wind blew within me. A stronger power surged through me, more powerful than I had ever felt on stage before. It was like a shock, electrifying me and our music. Even the crowd felt it and intensified their noise. It seeped into me, tingling through my body and soul. Then it became strongly familiar and all at once, I remembered.

I strained to look through the glaring lights and into the blackness but I couldn't see. And then one tiny ray of light darted from deep within the crowd, flying up, straight into my heart, and I knew. She was there, out there in the darkness somewhere. I took a deep, deep breath and I felt her light blend with mine and go all through me, spread through the stage, and fly out into the crowd.

They were on their feet screaming. Somehow, they knew, without ever having to know. My Earth started shaking with an overpowering love, a wonderment and a oneness. The woman who once opened my eyes, was out there, hiding in a mass of yelling, moving bodies, floating with their sound and noise. And I knew she was dancing. I could feel her life reach out to me. And together we danced, once more, me on the stage and her, far away, deep within the crowd. We twisted and spun the energy of the sky into the arena, weaving and playing with a sparkling illumination, one with life, dancing with the heartbeat of the world.

18

THE HEART OF THE WORLD

Late in October, just a week before writing *Darkness Into Light*, I had a truly amazing and beautiful dream. In the dream, I was walking in that now familiar dream tunnel when I came to an area that was completely made of crystals. The walls of the tunnel were composed of crystals and perfectly clear facets protruded, like diamonds, everywhere. Even the air seemed to sparkle inside this crystal cavern. I looked overhead and saw a hole in the tunnel's ceiling. The hole was a portal of light, encrusted with perfectly formed crystals.

I floated through the hole effortlessly and as I did, I felt a deep tingling in my body. My body seemed to get lighter and lighter as I floated up into a room that was filled with a brilliant white light. I felt enfolded and surrounded by the sparkling, moving, white energy. I floated in this wave of energy, feeling more and more relaxed. The feeling of relaxation melted into a sensation of freedom, which became a feeling of pure bliss. I really felt as though, by some alchemical magic, I was being transformed from flesh into light.

There were many people in the room, some were familiar and some appeared to be strangers. I felt as though I already knew Jason and Rosie when they came to take my hands in theirs. They both smiled with such warmth and welcome. The room was filled to the brim with an intense feeling of love and unconditional acceptance.

I took a deep, slow, wonderful breath and my body felt as though it were filling itself with light and love. I felt exhilarated as I seemed to draw in this warm, sparkling energy that surrounded me. I could hear, in the distance, delicate bells and ancient sounding chimes; and then a strange, dreamy, mesmerizing music seemed to move into the room, filling it with even more light and sound.

Jason and Rosie floated with me and around me, and we all beamed with happiness and laughter. Everyone in the room danced and floated on the rolling waves of beautiful music.

Later, when the story passed through me on to paper, I could feel that same joy and bliss, the dancing and the light. Even now, reading *Darkness Into Light* seems to trigger a cascade of mesmerizing feelings and faint, magical sounds, dream-like remembrances and visions.

I feel as though I have not fully remembered everything about those crystalline halls where everyone is still dancing. Sometimes I visit that place of light, in those spaces in between moments, that in the blink of an eye, are misplaced and forgotten.

It took me several weeks and numerous sessions to get this story on paper. Every time that I listened and typed, I could feel Jason and Rosie in the room with me. One night, as the story neared completion, I decided to quit for the night, tired of typing but not tired enough to sleep. I sat at my kitchen table, quietly sipping a cup of tea, while I waited for Rick to come home.

For just a brief moment I closed my eyes and immediately I could see them all dancing in pastel waves of motion. I could hear the steady beat of their music as the moment filled with the light and sound of that first, wonderful dream. I could feel myself moving slowly through a glistening field of energy. I felt as if I were being lifted into the sky to fly freely and joyously with their sounds.

Darkness Into Light brought me so many gifts, messages and new ideas. I felt that the story taught me more about energy, transformation and healing of the human spirit.

Rick and I struggled with this story and in our struggle with its symbols and meaning, we were pushed into a deeper healing and transformation of our own lives.

We could see that, in all of us, there is a constant struggle between darkness and light. The struggle is not between good and evil, but between ignorance and truth, fear and action, bitterness and trust, faithlessness and love. This constant struggle and conflict leads to moments of success and moments of falling. The success moves us toward truth. And yet, each time we fall, there is the opportunity to understand and change. From pain and despair we are born into light and hope and there is always hope. Darkness and light are both instruments of love that, in their contrast, move us toward illumination.

In the ancient traditions, shamans are described as the wounded warriors who, through their wounds and journeys into pain and fear, are able to see through the facades and illusions of the world. The shaman sees into the heart of the world, feels the beat of that heart, and knows the energy of the world.

In our fear and resistance, we often stay safely in the darkness. The darkness can be a place to hide. We linger at death's door, unaware of the transforming energy at our fingertips. The shaman pushes a person through his own darkness, through the dark wall of illusions, and into the light. The shaman, seeing the sea of transformational energy that flows through each moment and keen enough to see through the darkness, pushes a person to his symbolic death and then his rebirth into healing.

Rick and I have often discussed the shamanic nature of our own work with hypnosis. Hypnotic trance is a place in which we can fully experience and utilize light, darkness and that powerful balance point between the two forces in opposition. We have always had great respect for pain and despair in the process of transformation. We have each grown from our own experiences of pain and despair and learned most of what we know about the journey of healing from our own life experiences. *Darkness Into Light* greatly increased our knowledge and strengthened our convictions about the nature of healing.

There are shamans everywhere in our world, looking quietly from lofty windows, peering softly, breathlessly at the shimmering world of illusion, waiting patiently to turn darkness into light.

19

FROM *THE TIME TUNNEL:*

LOST IN THE REAL WORLD

I remember thinking, "Oh what a beautiful day! The sun is shining, the sky is blue, there's money in the bank, and everything's right with the world." I was filled with the gloriousness of the day. Lately I always felt this way, especially driving home in my new car, my baby.

This car was a gem, had every feature imaginable. My last car had been nice too, sun roof, tape deck, brand new. But this car was even better. I loved to settle down into the luxurious seat, pull very close to the steering wheel, and cruise gracefully down the highway. I felt powerful, serene.

And the car was gorgeous too, low to the ground and a bright, beautiful, rich-looking red, the color of bright red roses. "Yeah, this is where I want to be," I thought as I cut off the highway and glided through the streets of the town where I lived, streets busy with traffic, people rushing home from their day at the office.

I never rushed. I drove the car fast, it was a nice, high feeling to fly in my new car, but I often took the long way home. I was in no hurry. Joe would be waiting for me. Let him wait. I wouldn't let him spoil my joyous ride.

The town always looked the same. I looked at the buildings and the people as I rode through the streets. I knew they looked back, as the flashy, wine-colored car paraded past, driven by a rich-looking beauty! Who is that girl? I chuckled as their faces flew by.

Then, all of a sudden, but too slowly, I saw them up ahead. The awareness of the two bike riders, across the street, dawned gradually. I saw the boy on the red bike first. It looked so shiny and new. Red light, caught in the sharp glances of the bright, setting sun. The rider looked back at the boy behind him, shaking his curly brown hair. He looked at me and the steady stream of cars behind mine. Clearly wanting to cross, he swung out a little and in, and then out again. It was all over, in a flash of a moment, and yet, I felt as if I was watching the scene slowly, from some dream world.

I thought of stopping, almost wondering if I would, but then it was too late. I was too close. I sped by as the shiny, red bike pulled out once more. I judged it quickly and then I was past him. The fool swung out only inches behind me. I looked in the mirror and saw the car behind me come to a stop; a hand motioned them both to cross.

I breathed a little sigh. It hadn't really been close. I knew, instinctively, that the red bike was quick, he was daring, but I was quick too. I was too fast for a collision to find me.

Still, I felt a little embarrassed, nervous, a little like I wanted to hide ... How silly! There was no reason why I had to be the one to stop. Still, I looked at my face in the mirror and I wondered why I hadn't stopped. Why, at some quick moment, I had made the decision. ...I knew I would go on. It almost would have been easier to put my foot on that brake. I looked at the face of the driver behind me, tried to see his eyes, and I wondered.

I guess stopping just isn't me, it's not part of my life. My track is moving too fast and going straight up! I laughed off the flutter of remaining guilt. And then, as I turned off the main street, I turned abruptly into a small bird. He flew into my windshield and was jolted to the ground, in a flash, his small wings smashed along with his tiny life. It shocked me to a complete, frozen alertness, quickly awake, as a sad chill trickled down my spine. It had never happened to me before and I felt a little stunned.

I brought the brand new, shiny windshield wipers to life and looked away, as they washed off the splatter of a life lost. I looked at the sky as I pulled into the driveway. Yes, maybe it was going to rain tonight, after all.

Joe gave me the usual look as I walked in the door. "Took you long enough ... I'm starved! Wha'd you do, stop and see Maggie?"

"No, the traffic was terrible."

Same looks, same words, same faces. I was home and it felt too soon.

I turned the steaks over, dragging them through the juicy, bloody gravy. I was hungry too. I was so hungry!

I watched Joe sitting over his beer, lost in the moving, bright colors and the shiny energy of the television screen. I thought how right we had been to buy the more expensive set. It was nice to have the large screen, everything looked so real.

20

THE COFFEE BREAK

Lost In The Real World seemed to fly in from nowhere, and swoop down quickly into my life. After working nearly the whole month of November on *Darkness Into Light*, this story appeared and was finished in two days, taking me quite by surprise. In fact, even as I finished typing the story's last sentence, I had no idea that the story was coming to a close.

I sat at the typewriter, a stream of words, feelings and images flowing through me, and then, abruptly, the stream stopped, the words and images ceased to come. I felt that maybe I had lost my connection, had come up and out of my trance. And yet I felt very much in my trance, at just the perfect level, in just the right place. I waited and strained to hear the words, opened up to feel the sensations, but nothing came. Finally, I put the story aside and, still feeling a little confused, I decided I would try to continue the next day.

The very next night, I sat at my typewriter, ready to continue this new and intriguing story. I waited and waited but nothing happened. It must have been the perplexed and frustrated look on my face that prompted Rick, as he came in from work, to comment on my mood.

"Louisa, you look like you need a break ... why don't I make us some coffee." Rick was always careful not to interrupt me during writing, knowing how delicate the connection can be. But he sensed my frustration and my need to talk about it.

"I don't know what's happening ... this story seems stuck ... it won't move. This is the one I was telling you about last night. I thought I'd just continue with it tonight.

I think I am ready for a break. What do you think is happening?" I asked, hoping he might have a suggestion.

"Look, I know you don't like showing me stories before they're finished, but maybe, just this once, it will help." Rick was always eager to read my stories, even before they were finished. And maybe, just this one time, I needed some input, even before this story was complete.

Rick read the story and much to my surprise, he felt that the story was finished. I tried to tune in to the writers, as if to ask them if it were done. Their immediate answer was "yes, and you are both responsible for the name." I had never had the responsibility for naming a story before. But Rick had already heard the name in his mind. "Lost In The Real World, it feels right to me," he said, excitedly. It felt right to me, too.

Lost In The Real World is not only the shortest story that has come through, but it is also the most satirical. There is a biting, hard hitting quality to this story. Wondering how it would affect people, I introduced the story to my spiritual development class. I was amazed at the varied and exciting responses it evoked.

My reading of this story was followed by an animated discussion. We talked about ruts, routines and addictions. Some of my students talked about how mesmerizing material goals could become. We all recognized how we could find ourselves living from one material goal to the next. "When we finally get that new car or home ... then everything will be all right. Some day when I finally get what I want, then I'll sit back and read or learn or fulfill that deeper dream." We talked about the way in which our dreams, desires and intuitions get lost or misplaced in our fascination with the *real world.*

I think we are hungry for light, to be real, new, fresh, spontaneous, but we get lost in the glitter of shiny illusions and trapped in the dull sameness of our routines. We are lulled to sleep in our *real world* and the powerful, turbulent, creative nature of reality becomes submerged beneath the satiny surface of sameness. We give up our freedom in this world.

There are times when we collide with the world or the world collides with us. Some event tears at the fabric of our illusions and we are able to see deeper into our reality, feel feelings, doubts and questions. In those brief moments between routine and disaster, when our trance is disturbed by the unexpected, we get a chance to glimpse a flicker of light. These moments of light, of uncertainty, are exhilarating and sometimes unsettling, tenuous and frightening. We can choose to live in a world of wonder, power and freedom, or we can choose to become lost in the *real world*.

21

TWO SMOOTH STONES

During the first week in December, just after finishing *Lost In The Real World*, I began to feel the pull of approaching winter and the commotion of holidays as they seemed to tumble towards me. The hint and smell of winter in the air aroused the recluse in me. Part of me felt like a sleepy-eyed bear looking for a warm place to crawl into and hibernate.

But my ears pricked up at the crisp sounds of sleigh bells and carols and I could picture that huge sack of toys and memories and obligations and feelings and contradictions ... What an amazing time of year, such powerful remembrances and expectations.

Another important event marked this time for me, the last meeting of my spiritual development class, which was only days away. I had decided that we would break for the holidays and resume classes near the end of January and I wanted to do something special for this last class. I wanted to give my students a gift, a gift that would stimulate their thinking and intuition, a gift of love and learning from their teacher.

I sat down, one chilly evening, to meditate. I felt safe and warm in my heavy, soft robe, and my bedroom fit me like a tiny hermit's cabin, off in some secret woods. I hoped, perhaps, that I might be able to do some kind of psychic reading for the class, or that my guides might come through with a story that pertained to the class.

I drifted off quickly, into a wonderful trance, a trance filled with delicate images and swirling colors. And then amidst the images and colors, almost as if someone had suddenly turned on the sound, words came in slowly from the distance, like a string of gracefully flying geese, their sounds becoming gradually familiar. I picked up my pen to capture the words as they spiraled out of the sky and on to paper. I watched the words, as I began arranging them neatly in lines and verses, and only noticed when the process had finished, that it was a poem that had flown in, through me, and landed before my eyes.

It was such an elegant poem, such a joyous poem. It wove a web of delicate lines that connected together images and impressions of time and life. The poem, "We Meet Again," spoke to the continuity of life, the eternal nature of life, and reincarnation, the mechanism of eternal life. I could see that it spoke directly to the heart of the class, and yet it flew on into the heart of the world and life itself.

For various reasons, reincarnation had been the subject of discussion in a great many of our sessions together. A few of the class members, upon meeting one another, had had immediate and compelling sensations of "having known each other before." For others in the class, the experience of sitting together in a circle had created flashes of remembrance. At times, during our frequent meditations, various class members had strong "reincarnational" experiences that often shed light on some recurring feelings or dreams, or on some current life situation.

"We Meet Again" was a perfect poem for the class. The poem described to us what is perhaps the truth of reincarnation, that it is the expression of eternal life. The poem described the beauty and the process of reincarnation, without the dogma usually associated with a belief. It struck me that the poem seemed to describe the nature of reality in a way that, at least for me, expanded my description of reincarnation. The poem seems to describe the process of life's renewal and continuity as a constant seeking for truth, a dance of eternal transformation. And all along this path, we are full of wonder, always looking, maybe never knowing, "expressions of a beautiful radiance trying to see itself, find itself."

And our lively discussion touched often on this idea, that we might never know the answers. Listening to the flow of our opinions and speculations, it seemed to me that we all expected, at some point in this endless cycle of re-birth, to know, to understand. Even in a spiritual devel-opment class, where we are learning to trust our own intu-ition, there is still this dominant part of us that wants to know, expects to know. And this gentle poem seems to say, quietly, even happily, that perhaps this is not the goal. Perhaps it is the wonder, the living experience, the blessed opportunity to *be* infinite. I think that as we read and re-read this poem, we began, tentatively, to feel how much greater than knowing life, is being alive.

A few days after that last class meeting, and just moments after seeing one of my clients in the office, I sat back in the black leather recliner, the chair that my clients sit in. The leather grew warm from my body heat and my body relaxed into the soft, warm support of the chair. My senses drank in smells and sounds and as I drifted easily into trance, my eyes came to rest on a painting on the office wall. The beautiful painting, done by Pat Davidson, a friend of Rick's and mine, seemed to shine with a soft pink light. As I looked, the light seemed to resonate in me like a sound and for a moment, it felt as though so many others were seeing through my eyes and feeling the resonance of that light.

I reached for a pen, the words were coming again, sprinkling like droplets of spring rain, cool, soothing and alive. The poem was tentative at first, and then became more like a downpour as it flowed strong with inspiration and emotion. I could see it forming as a poem and I could feel the immediacy that I had felt, only days before, as the first poem came through.

Even before it was finished, I was wondering if these poems were coming from the same writers, if they were to replace the stories, or if they signaled some shift in my own awareness.

The storm of writing subsided, the clouds of questions parted, for the moment, and the light of this new poem shone through and touched me deeply. I read the words and lines that described the messages of my senses, descriptions of the room and its smells, and the light of that gentle painting, "hanging on the wall of my world."

I could see and feel, in a flash, that art, expression and the love that drives it, are passed on from soul to soul, and those works of art shoot forth rays of light that inspire and even connect two different worlds.

I thought of all the wonderful stories and of Pat's paintings and the songs that Rick writes. And I could see how each, in its own time, when least expected, passes on the spark of creation and lights a fire in another's heart or in another world.

The poem's name, "The Light of Intersecting Eyes," seems to describe perfectly the way in which light and inspiration are passed on and on.

The first two poems were the first of many poems to come. In December, five poems came through, and since then, there have been many more. Some have been filled with beauty and light. Some have spoken unabashedly of danger, human pain and suffering. Some have come as joyous greetings, some as warnings.

"We Meet Again" and "The Light of Intersecting Eyes," are two poems of joy and inspiration. They are like two smooth stones, soft and nearly translucent. Hold them gently in your hands and minds, and as you turn them over and over again, let them bring you peace and love.

22

We Meet Again

There is a breath, a moment, a change, and we begin again.
We dream, we look, some talk, some smiles,
friends on the scattered roads of time.
We stand in the green, tall as perfect trees.
Are they the same trees, old trees, only changed by time?
Has the strong, slow brush of the wind
changed our faces, covered our eyes?
There is a breath, a moment, a change,
and then we meet again.

Circles of trees, fingers reach out and form rings.
The lines of our hands curve,
Shaping cycles that move gently out,
like stones tossed into the water,
rippling out into a new world,
creating their patterns,
becoming liquid rings of gold.
There is a breath, a moment, a change, and we meet again.

Precious moments, things remind me, horizons beyond,
valleys of flowers.
Have we grown up together?
Do we hear the same rain?
Are we drowned in the same cleansing storms?
New worlds, old worlds, perfect worlds,
incomplete and urgent.
Where do we run to?
Roads turn, strangers pass by, forests of friends
being born, going home.
Seasons change, eyes remain, and there is always light.
Precious stones, do they jump, or are they pushed in by
    some unseen hand,

leaping happily, blindfolded, afraid to look,
knowing not to see.
There is a breath, a moment, a change, and we begin again.

Golden rings of light, thrown into new water,
sitting in a single, curving line,
every point equally distant from the center.
Round journeys, in the presence of our faces, again,
    courage again.
I used to think the day would come when I would know.
Does the circle begin? Where is its end?
And who are the lights surrounding me?
Faces of light, leaping, reaching out,
expressions of a beautiful radiance, trying to see itself,
find itself.
We share, we look together, pilgrims along the way.
A circle of light, sparks touching each other's souls,
creating a beautiful, healing fire,
reaching out to the season,
reaching out to the world, with a joyful light.
New worlds, old worlds, perfect worlds.
There is a breath, a moment, a change,
and then we meet again.

23

THE LIGHT OF INTERSECTING EYES

Falling into softness,
strong black leather, of a watchful chair,
caresses my body, my being.
Resting a head against this chair of delight,
eyes, gliding upward, focused on a visionary art,
glances caught on a golden, pink sky.
Paintings of water, of light,
a scene hanging on the wall of my world,
a window to another world, resting dreamily.
A pink light drifts gracefully through the sky.

Strong scents of sharp, orange tea.
A room alive with the argyle forms of a distant world.
Mirrors reflect artist,
reflections on the face of a white wall.
Diamond shaped patterns, woven into other worlds,
intersecting lights in unseen eyes.
Hearts touched by her glow,
her presence, her silvery mettle.
This pink light drifts gracefully through the sky.

Her heart lives in her paintings,
images of pink, mixed with gold,
lifting a new sky, reaching up,
appreciation of soothing shadows,
colors applied to the surface
and deeper,
pigments of glossy oils,
she dresses the world with.
Her pink light drifts gracefully through the sky.

The aroma of images reaches out.

She has taught me,
art goes on,
affects dreams,
instills, touches,
yields the fruit of a divine courage,
forever, no beginning, no end.
A pink light drifts endlessly through the sky.

A vision of feelings producing effects.
The making of things of form, of beauty.
Born under the wings of Artemis,
a goddess of the moon, shine reaches out from her orb,
and touches the reverie of the world.
A pink light drifts gracefully through the sky.

She will paint worlds with her oils,
with her words, with her ways.
In a flash of a moment, another sees, a rhyme is told,
odes written,
a gift passed on to the world.
An artist hears and sings, lyrical notes of joy.
Another spark passed on.
The light of intersecting eyes creates paintings,
filled with the spark of the Divine.
A pink light drifts gracefully through the sky.

24

PRELUDE TO A PARTY

January appeared like a door, waiting to be pushed open into a brand new year. The past year had been filled with surprises and intense discoveries. It sometimes seemed to me that I had been inundated with changes and difficult new ideas. Even after all the turmoil, the new year seemed pregnant with possibilities. As I stood tentatively at its threshold, I wasn't sure that I was ready to push on that door and enter.

On New Year's Eve, with only hours to go before the new year, I sensed that my spirit guides were close by and that the conditions were right for some communication with them. I think they sensed that Rick and I were feeling apprehensive and a little tired. I sat down to meditate and within moments their message came through. The message and an accompanying poem really lifted both Rick and me, as we prepared to attend a New Year's Eve party with friends.

As I look back now, that short message was the spark of inspiration that helped us to push, with enthusiasm, on that door of newness. We entered the new year with more hope and inspiration, ready to create positive outcomes from the host of possibilities.

Later that week, I met someone named Sarah, in a dream, and her story, *An Ordinary Door*, began to open and unfold. At first glance this story did seem very ordinary. But then I've seen that doors to change and awakening are often deceptively ordinary. They hide in our routines, waiting for us to turn the handle and walk through.

I felt Sarah's feelings, every one of them, as I wrote down her story for you. I felt as though I was inside her mind and body and it was the feelings that fascinated me most. The feelings came as they would come in anyone's life, one after the other and in waves, sometimes in conflict with her thoughts or beliefs. I knew, as she had the courage to feel her feelings, that each feeling moved her more and more towards change. I sensed that there were times when she could have blocked a feeling, or gotten lost in thinking, or refused her own urges and dreams, but she didn't. As she shares with you this most intimate of stories, listen closely to the power of feelings and the progress of dreams. Let Sarah inspire you to push on the ordinary doors in your life.

Rick and I would also like to share with you a personal message, sent to us from our spirit guides, on the eve of the new year. The message inspired us greatly, and confirmed for us some of our speculations. The message lifted us both into the new year, on a wave of energy and purpose.

Following the New Year's Eve message, is the story, *An Ordinary Door*, the first story of a new, and not so ordinary, year.

25

A New Year's Eve Message
From Our Guides

"I come to you with great delight, on this joyous eve, a night on the verge of a change, a new beginning in the fragments of earthly time, a powerful time, for much power and strength can be ingested into newness, beginnings created, and yes, a time to be full of laughter, of merriment.

"I come to you with humility, the eagerness to continue our work, and some little trepidation, the uncertainty of the beginnings of our momentous task ahead.

"I come, partly, in answer to your questions. I am only one of many, but I am the poet who joins with many to help write the so aptly named, *Songs That Drift Back To Us.* [This is the working title that Rick and I were using for this book at the time.] And I am also the very same poet who will join you in the creation of a tony book of verse I will refer to as *Holes in the Wall of Time,* because it is just exactly that which will enable us to make physical our creation. You may call the book of our odes what you wish, however, I bestow upon you that freedom.

"Other artists will join us from time to time, (ha ha, shall we let them? You will say yes, I know!) but the majority of our work of poems will fall on the two of us. I will give you my verse, my thoughts, and you will step through our hole and retrieve words, pulling them gracefully through to your world, no small feat indeed. And together our talents and the talents of others will mesh, forming a silver chain, flowing into many worlds. The result, two divine books, with a view made available only from the corners of time. And many more books to come;

the worlds are filled with the songs of artists, waiting to be written.

"My name you will hear someday if you listen. I once had an earthly name, known to many, and many more names since. But who I am will not be a part of these verses. They will belong to time, and rightly so, not personalities, not I nor you. We may only carry the words and tales, lovingly. But we will leave a tiny imprint of our care upon the pages and that small imprint will shine into the hearts of many.

"Your new year will be a year to sing and dance and make merry, for you and our beloved one called Rick. The fruits of your labors are growing into the most beautiful, ripe fruit imaginable. This new year will be a year of harvesting that fruit, picking spiritual apples of intense light, and the golden apples of the physical world you both so richly deserve. I take great joy in knowing that the sweet juice from these fruits will flow into the lives of many, and many will share in your abundance.

"As your group of writers and many loving souls gather here to wish you, Louisa and our estimable song-master, Rick, the brightest of New Years, I give you this, my first letter to you both. Yes I am the writer of many things; you have heard my songs before, I see them in your files, ha ha!

"And now I give you our first ode of your new year, a blessed year. I know you share these words with me, Louisa."

First Night Song For The Planet Earth

My gift will be my voice
one sound, calling, I promise to sing.
I have seen light, and know
there will be no more silent nights
for any of us.
Voices cry out in the darkness,
and flames of light sing forth
their fiery songs of strength, in answer.

It is all there to see.
Who will hear silence lifting away,
holes in the wall of time,
where the voices of warriors can be heard.
Join with me, and listen with joy,
songs for the planet Earth.

———•—•———

"I go now, my blessings to you both. In the days ahead, there will be flashes of moments when you will both hear my laughter and we will all smile together. Someday, in the silence, you will hear all our names but for now, we send you our combined love and the knowing that in the first breath of the New Year, we will be with you, sending you our laughter, our joy and our love."

26

FROM THE TIME TUNNEL:

AN ORDINARY DOOR

I woke up slowly, not wanting to move, reluctant to budge from under the warm blanket; it was too cold. I could feel the coolness of the room against my face, forcing me deeper under the covers.

Oh well, it was Saturday, there was no hurry. Today was my day of rest, my free day. Cousin Annie would be coming soon to give Tom his breakfast, read to him, spend the day with him. Aahh, a free day for me! Or was it? Are any days we live really free? I really didn't know what to do with my free days anymore. I would sleep a little later, that was all. Allow myself to loll in bed for a longer time, but sometimes nothing else ended up being very different.

I pulled the blankets up to my nose but I was awake. I could hear the crows dancing on the roof over my head and I wondered if they were cold too. They were tapping and strutting on the roof, almost as if they were trying to get my attention.

All right, birds, I'm awake! What should we do today? Should we fly off to some warm Caribbean island, and walk aimlessly by the green waters? Or perhaps to the Orient for tea. Or shall we go shopping in Paris? Will you take me on your dark wings to the Champs Élysées? Some other day? Oh well, shopping is probably a good idea. There is Marlena's party coming up and it's time I had a new dress. Something red ... or black, you say? Well let's go see.

I hopped out of bed, in a burst of hopefulness. Some-how though, wiggling my toes into faded slippers brought me back to Earth. I went to open the door for Annie.

"You still here, Sarah, I thought you'd be gone by now ... I do have my key, you know. You don't have to wait for me every Saturday, you know," Annie grumbled, as she pulled herself up the stairs and in through the worn, tired door.

"I know, I thought I'd wait for you and we could have some tea before I go out."

"Where are you about today, girl?" Annie searched my face.

"I don't know, maybe shopping." I wondered, briefly, what answer she was looking for.

"Sarah, you've got to make a life of your own. It's a good Christian thing, what you feel for your brother, but you can't do any more for him. You've got to find your own life, friends, maybe even a suitor. You're a pretty girl; you should have suitors. Your mother'd say that, if she were here, so I'm saying it to you ... otherwise you'll end up like me, taking care of your Aunt Emily for fifteen years ... Now I can't walk too well and I'm alone, except for you and Tom. I lived with Emily for forty years, and I wish I'd walked through that door, when I was young and pretty, and kept on walking."

"Oh, Annie, no you don't ... you always say that. You and Aunt Emily were good for each other, and besides, what would she have done without you?"

"She would have lived the exact same life for herself ... but I ... aahh," she sighed, "I would have seen Paris." Annie was lost in some other world. "Someday you'll know, Sarah, when I hope it's not too late."

I knew it was time to leave; anything was better than listening to Annie talk about what might have been. Besides, it was different for me, Tom was all I had and I was all he had, now that our parents were gone. There was no one but me to help him, to distract him from the crippling prison he lived in. Yes, Annie came on Saturdays, but there was no one else but me to walk through his door of confinement on Sunday through Friday. Besides, I was getting out in the world, a little; I had the part time job, two days a week, now, at the nursing home, and I had friends there. Marlena had even asked me to her party; maybe I would even go.

Taking the bus into the city was like stepping into another world. Over the bridge and through the door and into a world filled with people hurrying through madly lit streets. Blank faces, busy mouths, fast feet; were these creatures of my world? No, I think I just landed here, sometimes, mostly on Saturdays.

I walked around the city, feeling so good to be aimless. I wondered if freedom felt like this. When I'd walked enough, I found my usual lunch spot. As I walked through the door of the tiny cafeteria, I could smell my usual hot dog waiting for me, yellow mustard floating through the air, meeting my nose at the door. But today was different, on this Saturday afternoon, I could smell pickles too. So green and fresh, the aroma cut through the heavy air and spread a crisp newness over the room. Suddenly, today seemed different. I ordered a hot dog with my pickles, for the first time.

After lunch, I wondered if I should start heading back ... without the dress ... but no, I wasn't ready to make that decision, not yet. I would look at dresses first and then I would decide not to go to the party.

I loved looking at store windows. I passed slowly by each beautiful glass, filled with women who went to parties, lifeless bodies that shopped in Paris, red lips that drank tea in the Orient, masks of perfect women, shining out through the glass, mannequins who would come to life when I went home to my cold house. I had the feeling they would shatter the glass and parade on the street laughingly, when all the real dummies went home.

I walked slowly towards the bus stop, pausing only when a beautiful woman in a black dress beckoned to me from her beautiful glass cage. She had yellow hair, like mine, and she stood silently in a glaze of black satin, ready to move; motionless, but ready to spring to life, a life of excitement, style, black satin.

I stood in front of her window, lost in her world, until a little girl, tugging at my fingertips, awakened me. "You have pretty hair," she pointed up at me. She couldn't have been more than four or five; her cute eyes studied me intently. I couldn't help but smile and return the compliment. "I wish I had your pretty golden curls." My fingers touched her soft, curly hair, and we both smiled. Her small hands reached out and grabbed my hair. "Pretty, yellow," she said seriously. "What's your name," she questioned, as mommy appeared and pulled her away. "Sarah," I answered laughingly.

"She's right, you know, you have the most beautiful yellow hair I've ever seen, Sarah," a deep male voice surprised me!

"I bet you say that to every blond you see!" Startled, I wondered that any words appeared in my mouth.

"No, I have to admit, you're the only woman I've ever said that to." He smiled so gently, a tall figure, unmoving, appearing abruptly in the doorway of my world. "You should wear black with that hair, satin ... yes, you are a woman who would shine in satin, a woman who would shine in any room." His eyes were unmoving, staring at me with an intensity I'd never seen. "Actually, I can see your beauty would make any color pale, any dress fade in your light. But just to be sure, I want to see you in every color, in every light imaginable." His eyes were warm and filled with a sincere softness.

"Does this mean you're going to be a part of my life, from now on?" I laughed jokingly with a joyous nervousness.

"Just try and stop me. I want to see what that yellow hair looks like, every moment ... all the ordinary moments, and all the seconds of excitement, and with you, I have a feeling that they'll always be one and the same." He talked with a confidence that was both unsettling and hopelessly endearing. "Take this card and write your number on it, Sarah, my hands are shaking far too much." He pressed his business card into my hand. But instead of writing, I ran, fled through the crowd, gripped with a sudden fear, a sudden feeling that someone had stepped too far in through the door of my world. And the crowd responded by folding in around me, covering me, protecting me with a wall of people.

The handsome stranger was gone.

On the bus, I turned the card over and over in my hand. A banker's card, how funny, I thought all bankers were old and stuffy, not handsome with soft brown eyes and gentle smiles.

"You're early again." Annie looked at me critically, as I pulled myself up the stairs, and in through the old, worn door. "I thought you'd be out, at least, until seven."

Tired, all at once, I slid into the kitchen chair and looked up at the large, brown, familiar clock, high on the wall, really too high to see.

"Well I'll be going, then ... shall I see you the same time next Saturday ... any plans?" Annie recited, as she backed through the door.

"Thank you, Annie ... yes, next Saturday, I have to pick up a dress I'm going to order for Marlena's party."

"A dress, Sarah?"

"Yes, Annie, just an ordinary dress ... black satin."

27

THE ANDROID WOMAN

Towards the end of January, I could still feel my enthusiasm for this new year building, and at the same time I began to feel the need for order and organization. Our private practice was swelling with people, heartened and strengthened by the new year, and eager to make progress on personal goals. There were also people to whom I had promised private readings, who were patiently waiting to be scheduled. It was a time filled with cross currents of activity and in need of some skillful management.

While busily shopping, one afternoon, I noticed the Valentine's Day card display and immediately thought of Rick. It struck me that perhaps, this year, I would be a bit more organized than usual, and buy Rick's card early. I mused over the cards, looking at the pictures, and reading all the various messages of love. I finally picked one card that was very romantic and worded beautifully. As I was leaving, another card caught my eye, a very curious card. On the cover was a silver skinned android woman. There was something irresistible about the way she glistened coolly, in luminescent tones of silver and blue. Rick so often says, jokingly, that I spend more time in other worlds and other times than I do here on Earth, in the present. It seemed like the perfect card to give to Rick from his otherworldly wife, so I bought it as a second, humorous card.

Days later, I began to think about a Valentine's present. My mind seemed blank until I remembered that Rick had requested, just before Christmas, that maybe I could channel a story for him, as a present. The time before Christmas was a blur, and didn't lend itself to quiet writing, but now, with two weeks to go before Valentine's Day, surely I could find the time for a Valentine's story.

There was only one problem with this plan of action. I had never asked the *writers group* to write a story for a specific person or about a particular subject. Yet many of the stories did seem to come through in response to some personal question or dilemma. I resolved to try this direct approach and see if the *writers group* would respond.

I sat down the very next evening for a good long meditation. I asked the *writers group* to write a story specifically for Rick. I could feel them there, in the night air, a loving, creative presence of energy and wisdom, sparkling just beyond my vision, coming together in that space that was so close to me and so incredibly distant, all at the same time. Though they were just beyond ear shot, I knew that they were talking and laughing, though I heard nothing. The typewriter sat there silently, switch on, red lights like tiny beacons in the darkness. I sat there for quite some time. I knew that they were responding, I could feel it, but I could not hear their words. I finally turned off my trusty typewriter and went to bed.

The week before Valentine's Day passed uneventfully. The evening before the holiday, I signed my cards for Rick, and planned to leave for the store to buy something silly, like a chocolate heart. I had all but given up on getting something from the *writers* when I glanced at the silvery blue figure on my card and immediately, I knew there would be a story. I grabbed my note pad and pen, barely in time to catch the words that came flowing and tumbling into my mind. I wrote the words they sent to me and then typed them so they would be legible. The writing had been fast, scribbled and squeezed on to margins, with not a space to breathe, punctuate or attend to spelling. Just after midnight, on Valentine's Day morning, the *writers* and I finished *When Worlds Collide*.

Though I had originally asked for a story for Rick, the *writers* gifted me with a beautiful story for the both of us. This story is dedicated to Rick, though it is also a Valentine's Day present from one world to another. From my writers to Rick and me and everyone who reads these words.

28

WHEN WORLDS COLLIDE

8011 stared hard through the glass, fixing her silver eyes intently on her world. It was a beautiful, gleaming sight, the city she saw below her, from the window. Thousands of tall, shining buildings pointing sharply towards the sky, all metal, stark structures picking up cool lights from very distant stars.

8011 stood there sadly, for a long time, eyeing her world. 8017 found her, sometime later, looking out into the darkness.

"Darling what is wrong? I've never seen you look like this!"

"I'm fine 8017 ... No, I'm not fine. I am very sad," she said softly.

"Sad, that's impossible! There is absolutely nothing to be sad about. Besides, no one in our world ever gets sad." He looked at her with total disbelief.

"But I am sad. I'm sorry 8017, I know I am when I look out of the window, and I can't seem to stop looking."

Darling One-One, what are you seeing? There is nothing but perfection out there. We are so lucky, we live in a perfect world, a city of total beauty. Why look ... Just look at how the sharp angles of the buildings pick up the starlight, and reflect off each other in the darkness. Tell me you've seen a more beautiful sight!"

"I have, that is the problem ... I think."

"There is no place, no world, that could be as perfect and as beautiful as ours. We have everything here we could ever want. Look at the great numbers of people who come to visit our world, year after year, and look at the

162 RICK & LOUISA CLERICI

large amount who stay, who decide they don't want to leave. We lack for nothing. Even our atmosphere is perfect; it is cool here, year round. The misty light is the same all year round. Why ... nothing changes; we live in a world of constant perfection. Why even our bodies are perfect. Look at our smooth, even lines, the clearly defined angles and edges of our joints, the fine, sharp, pointed fingers we have, the steady regular gaze of our eyes. Our bodies, even, are perfection."

"No, I don't think so One-Seven, at least I don't think so anymore. Even our bodies lack something; something is missing from our world."

"What? What could there possibly be that we lack, One-One ... and why do you think this?"

"I went into the tunnel, last night again, and I saw it One-seven; I know what is missing."

"Oh no, One-One, not again. You know it is not advised!"

"But I had to ... I heard her calling me ... she was somehow aware of my sadness ... she wanted to help me."

"This is highly irregular, and you know this, One-One. And who ... who is it that wants to help you?"

"I met her, One-Seven, and I'm getting to know her ... and him. You know who I speak of ... our links."

"Oh no, not this parallel life idea again ... One-One, you know I'm not sure I think this is true ... why would we want to see our parallel life? There could be nothing there for us, One-One, we have everything here, I tell you."

"No, One-Seven, I know that is not true ... I have gone through their door and I have seen. She and her partner have told me. There is something there. They call it "to feel," and it is beautiful, One-Seven ... if you only knew ... if you only knew how glorious it is. I have seen them do it, "to feel" and "to sense." She has told me all about it. She says sometimes it seems like it is not worth it. Sometimes it is so very hard. Sometimes it hurts. But at times, it is wonderful! At times, they feel something called "joy," and oh, One-Seven, it is truly wonderful ... I felt it, I felt it for a moment, and it was so ... so indescribable ... aahh, if you

could only feel it! They also have something called "love."
It is the most wonderful feeling there is, One-Seven, more
beautiful than anything we have here ... and I felt it too, I
really did. But, you know, I have felt it once here too, One-
Seven, the day of our meeting. I want to go to their world,
One-Seven, they have what is missing from this place."

"What are you saying, One-One? You ... you are disturbing me!"

"Disturbing you, One-Seven? What is that? What is
disturbing ... what is it like?"

"I ... I don't know ... it is strange."

"No, it is not strange, One-Seven. It is truly beautiful ...
you are "feeling" something. You are like me, One-Seven,
you are ready, ready now to leave this place, to make the
transition."

"But no ... I don't know ... how ... how could this
happen?"

"They know of us, One-Seven, and they will know of
us more, us and all our experiences of this world. We can
be absorbed into their world. It is not too difficult, if we are
truly ready. She will absorb me. Her name is Louisa. Even
their names are so different ... no numbers, so blank and
regular ... but even their names seem to have feelings.
Louisa, I like it, it has a sound that feels beautiful. And
your link, One-Seven, Richard, is a name that feels so
strong and wise. I like them so much and you will too,
One-Seven! I know it, you will like the links that we will
join. You will even know what it feels like, to "like." You
will like us, One-Seven."

"I ... I don't know ... One-One ... I ..."

"Come here, One-Seven, and look out of this window
again. Look at our world, one last time, and remember,
remember it well. Someday we may want to again think of
this place. It has been important that we looked from this
window, that we were here; we have learned so much, as
so many learn here. It is a good place, One-Seven, but it is
time to experience new things."

One-Seven looked out at the cold world that now
began to look like his home and then he looked quietly at

One-One. He watched, incredibly, as something liquid seemed to come out of One-One's silvery eyes and move slowly down her strong metallic face. Something happened then, something seemed to move inside him. At first there was a slight sound and then a feeling seemed to melt and fuse and to slowly come to life inside his cold alloy of a body.

One-One's mouth smiled and her lips seemed to have a bright redness that he had never noticed before.

"Please hold my fingers, 8017," and 8011 moved her squeaky, metal joints, pointing them towards him, and they joined hands.

And there was a flutter, as feelings awakened and danced through their cold metal tubes and silver hearts, two bodies beginning to feel a new warmth.

"This is love, 8017," she said, as she felt something begin to pound inside of her.

"It is wonderful, 8011," he said, with a new voice, filled with feeling. "Yes it is time."

And on one very cool night, the tunnel between worlds was very, very busy. And on the planet Earth, two bright stars, soon to shine with even more light, celebrated St. Valentine's Day. And outside their window, two silver butterflies approached a new world. They danced and flew and awakened to a life filled with the feelings of love.

29

FLOWERS IN A FIELD

Valentine's Day dawned softly for the two of us. The morning sun filtered brightly through blinds and split into vivid colors as it pierced the hanging crystal spinning slowly in the window. Rainbow pieces danced a slow wistful dance across the walls and ceiling, shimmering like light reflected on water. It was as if we awoke to a room already in silent, colorful celebration. I thought of the silver butterflies and couldn't wait to give Rick his new story from another world.

As I got up to put some coffee on, I made just enough noise so Rick would think he was waking naturally. When I returned to bed with two steaming cups, Rick was already sitting up, eager to see this new tale, having heard me typing well into the night. Though Rick had said it many times, I could see how the stories had fit so perfectly into his life, bringing to him an excitement and a spiritual adventure, long awaited. As I slipped back into bed with coffee in hand and the story tucked under my arm, Rick beamed with a readiness to continue the journey.

Rick read with the excitement of a child to whom stories are so much more than writing, but more like passageways and crawl spaces filled with magic and meaning. He loved 8011 and 8017, and in a gesture of welcome, he held his arms open. "We welcome you to our world, a world of feeling ... Can you feel them? I think that they're right here in the room, merging with us. They must be our link to another dimension, a dimension of existence that's more about form and function and cool detachment. And I think it's a place we all visit from time to time, when *to feel* becomes too much, and we need a little distance. It's like having guests from another country who, in their excitement, help you to remember the beauty of your own land."

When I gave Rick the card with the cool blue, android woman on the cover, we laughed until we cried. Rick said that was just how he had pictured 8011, and he couldn't take his eyes off her.

There was something mesmerizing about her and the way she looked back from the distance of a greeting card, and the way she seemed to look straight into my heart, seemed to know my heart, a heart I sometimes feared and fought with, a heart she longed for.

It was a very busy time for us, that Valentine's Day, and maybe because of that hectic pace, something very special took place. I felt as though a part of me was tired of feeling the pressure of the world. I wanted to escape and I think that for a time, perhaps only a moment, I did.

Some would say that a part of me gave birth to 8011, or maybe some part of me merged for a time with 8011 and her world of gleaming perfection. I guess I needed to experience that world without feelings.

Before this story came to life, 8011 and I had been communicating in the dream tunnel. It was the kind of communication of which I was only marginally conscious. When the story came through to me, just a glimmer of our meetings emerged from my deepest memory. She was my link to another world, she is a part of me and I a part of her.

I think, as I look at all the evidence and clues before me, that we are beings of many dimensions, multi-dimensional beings. I think that as we evolve spiritually we become more and more aware of these other parts of ourselves, merging the dimensions, becoming more aware of our wholeness. Perhaps, as we awaken, we are all like silver butterflies, flying from one world to another as though they were flowers in a field, lighting on one and then another with great awareness and passion.

30

THESE ARE YOUR FEELINGS

The end of February turned bitter cold. The wind whipped and rustled, churning up swirls of snow and waves of emotion. There seemed to be a rawness in the air and in my heart. Somehow, perhaps due to my encounters with 8011 and 8017, I was feeling closer than ever to my feelings.

At times I felt swept away by my love for Rick. There was a sweetness and warmth that touched me in so many of my moments. Tears of joy and appreciation would well up in my eyes, just at the sound of Rick's voice. I always felt a deep love for Rick but these emotions seemed to have a life of their own.

I knew that Rick was feeling this shift too. Though most often calmer than I, Rick was always close to his feelings and trusted them deeply. Yet I could see in his moods and actions that he was feeling an unusual emotional charge. We were both very sensitive and vulnerable, at this time, and luckily we realized it, especially in our relating to each other.

All of my emotions were heightened during this shift, not only love, but also anger and pain. I found that, consequently, I could not watch the news, because of the storms of feelings that rose up in me in response to many of the stories and their accompanying film footage. Rick and I discussed this turning away from the news media. I felt a little guilty about it, as though I was somehow obligated to witness the events of the world. Rick said, "Remember, the news is not what is new in the world, but what is most riveting, ugly, frightening and gory. The news is not a window on the world ... it's big business, very big business. It is in the business of entertaining, not informing.

There are a billion beautiful things happening each moment, all over the world, even in the most devastated places, but it's not considered newsworthy." Even knowing this, Rick tended to watch the news more than I did, although I often heard him turn the TV off in disgust, long before the show was over.

I shifted my TV viewing to the educational channel, in search of more enriching shows and a little quieter entertainment. Of course I found myself watching a show that explained, in amazing detail, the destruction of the Amazon Rain Forest and the depletion of the ozone layer, with all the projected consequences for the planet Earth and humankind. Rick returned that night from a music rehearsal to find me crying, on the couch, in rage and pain. He held me for a long, long time, and watched the rest of the show with me. When I looked up at his face, I saw that he was crying too.

I wanted to fly through a cool forgiving space to a planet of flawless perfection, where everything gleamed and glistened, and even the air flowed in quiet measured breaths. But somewhere, beneath the storm of emotions, I could still hear a small voice that whispered to me softly, "These are *your* feelings ... they are essential to your wholeness and to your full experience of life." I could feel that too, and it moved me as truth and feelings move us.

During those last weeks of February, I began taking the dream journeys that led to the place and people in my next story. As I met this young woman, Rosemary, and saw through her tear-filled eyes, I could immediately understand her, as though she were speaking a language that I had truly begun to learn and know. I also realized that I been prepared, over the course of the past few weeks, for an experience of love and pain of incredible depth.

It took me several weeks to finish channeling this story. I cried softly on many nights; at times the pain was unbearable. The truth in this story is simple and unadorned. There is an innocence that is disarming. Stay close to your feelings and let them lift you into knowing as you read *The Wings Of His Eyes*.

31

FROM *THE TIME TUNNEL:*

THE WINGS OF HIS EYES

The news came on a warm Saturday in June. It was just an average, routine, very warm Saturday afternoon. I was startled, I remember, actually much more than startled; I was shaken, shaken hard to my very core.

It took me a long time to replace the receiver on my phone. I held the cold, black handle for what seemed like forever, dazedly listening to the loud hum of a line disconnected, allowing the noise to blend with the screeching inside of me, not wanting it to come out, not yet; and slowly it became an alarm, pulsing in my shaky hands. As I pushed the phone down then, quickly into its cradle, I knew it was an alarm I would never forget.

I sank down further into my scratchy chair, trying to retreat, trying to forget, trying to remember. I began reviewing the room, almost as if something had changed. It seemed different. It was almost as if it had been one very certain room, before the call came, and now it was different; something had changed. I looked carefully at each piece of furniture. The two beige and blue chairs still rested gingerly on the oriental flowers, hiding in the carpet. My keys slept idly on the table where I had casually thrown them to rest the night before. The blue velvet sofa eyed me quietly, regally, as always.

Everything was exactly the same. But somehow, everything looked out of place. The yellow marigolds I had brought home yesterday were definitely too bright, too fresh, and the sharp crystal of the vase seemed to pick up too much light from the window and sparkle far, far too much. I glanced at the clock and it had stopped, yes, I had thought that, at the time. It can't possibly be only one o'clock; it must be nighttime. I know hours and hours have gone by, days, minutes, lifetimes.

No, not a moment has passed and nothing has changed. Everything in the room is the same, except my hands. The left hand that held the phone receiver trembled with a violent uncertainty, hands shaking with a feeling I had never known before.

What about the view from my window, could that be what was different, I wondered? I was at home on this fifteenth floor, and most at home with the vision coming from my window. It gave me a relaxing feeling to be high above the busy streets of the city, removed from the world. But as I walked to the window, I realized that it was indeed my window that was different, the only thing that had changed besides my hands.

With a piercing shiver that went all through me, I realized that the view had changed totally, had changed quickly. I don't know why, but I felt in that moment that I was much closer to the ground. I could see all the people on the street so clearly; all their actions seemed so detailed. I could almost hear each individual cry, I felt so close to them. My view had changed drastically. I was closer to the world, and for the first time in my life, I could really see.

The rest of the day was a slow, vacant blur. I made a few calls, started to pack, but mostly I just sat, holding on to visions, visions of Peter, scenes of summer days far away.

I had to smile as I remembered the day I saw him for the first time, back on the old farm in Indiana, the most beautiful place in the world. I was nine, and Peter was only a year older.

I had arrived at the farm with my parents, after a long trip. I remember how pretty my mother looked in the new hat she had bought for this occasion. I'll never forget that hat, it was so big, the straw was so light, almost a lemon color, and there were two luscious, pink roses draped elegantly across the crown; they were so vibrant, they looked real. I thought it was the most beautiful hat I had ever seen.

My father and I were so tired; he was tired of driving and I was tired of sitting. But mother seemed fresh, not tired in the least. Her face was radiant, framed by the garden of a hat, and her eyes were filled with a liquid joy, the joy of seeing her best friend, a woman she hadn't seen in nine years.

The farm looked bigger than any place I'd seen, and so different, but I still didn't want to be there. I wanted to be back in New York with all my friends from school. Now I would miss a whole summer of our escapades, ballet classes, and all the millions of things we had planned for the summer. I already missed my best friend, Pam. I couldn't believe I wouldn't see her again until September. Why September was a lifetime away! I wondered if she would still remember me when I got back.

My mother and her friend, this strange lady I was now supposed to call Aunt Helen, were ecstatic. My father seemed happy too, he talked to my new Uncle Bob and he looked relaxed, his face didn't look like it always did, back home.

We all sat at the biggest table I had ever seen, it looked big enough to seat a million people, and we had a huge meal. So much food, fresh corn that tasted sweet, and Aunt Helen let me eat with my hands, dripping butter as I went along. And huge, puffy, red tomatoes, and for dessert we had strawberries that Aunt Helen had picked that morning, bright red berries, totally immersed in a thick, white cream. I watched as, every once in a while, one of the juicy, vigorous strawberries would fight through the cream and rise slowly to float to the top. I played with my bowl until I tasted just one and I can still remember the taste.

I sat facing two of my cousins. Bobby Jr. was fifteen and Henry was sixteen, and they were immediately bored with me and I was immediately very bored with them. I think it was the only time in my life that I wished I was not an only child. What a boring summer this was going to be, no girls around, and three older, horrid, male cousins. I hadn't met the third cousin yet, but he was a boy too, and I was sure he wouldn't be any better. I wished I could go home.

I remember when my father asked, "Where is Peter? I'm sure Rosemary can't wait to meet him!" ("Yuk," I thought to myself, "I can't wait for this summer to be over.")

Aunt Helen let out a sigh that came often to her. "Oh, he's probably out in the fields somewhere; it's hard getting Peter inside long enough for meals, sometimes. Why don't you boys take Rosemary out to meet him, if you search, I'm sure you'll find him somewhere, and you can give your cousin a tour of the farm."

My new cousins looked at each other and then at me, all of our eyes blinking looks of disgust in unison, and off the three of us went.

"You're probably scared of cows, huh, Rosemary?" Bobby Jr. said, with a large grin on his face. "Bein' from the city and all, have you ever seen a cow?"

"Yes," I said defiantly, "I've seen millions of cows ... we saw a movie at school."

"Ha," Henry and Bobby Jr. thought this was just so funny. "Well, these are the cows, here over the fence," they laughed, as I looked too amazed at being that close to a very real cow. "You can probably find Peter out there somewhere in the cornfields, when you get tired of looking at cows, but we have things to do now," Bobby laughed as they quickly pushed me over the fence, into the midst of the cows, and both of them ran in the opposite direction, laughing as hard as two young devils could.

As I sat facing my first real cow, I looked straight into her big brown eyes and wished more than anything in the world, to go home! I think she understood; her eyes looked at me with gentle softness and we became immediate friends, my first friend on the farm, but as it turned out, not my only one.

I sat with the cows for a while; I watched them and they watched me, and then I climbed over the fence and started walking. It felt nice to be alone. I was glad my horrible cousins had gone, and I was glad I didn't have to listen to the grown-ups talk, on and on. Even though I definitely didn't like this horrid farm, I had to admit, being by myself, here, free to run around, was kind of nice. I listened to the hum of the bees, and kept walking.

I followed a path away from the farmhouse and found myself facing a very large field, a field that seemed to stretch as far as the eye could see in every direction, and it was full of greens and golds, tall grass lit by a strong sun. My first sight of corn growing in a field was something I've never forgotten; till this day I can see that picture in my mind. Millions of ears of corn, all gently moving with a slight breeze. Golden sunny streaks, dancing everywhere with the greens and browns, making the field vibrant and alive with a fire all its own. And in the middle of this yellow field was a head of yellow hair sticking out, brighter than all the ears of corn. From where I stood, I could just see the top of Peter's head.

He looked at me so curiously as I walked through the tall corn, towards him. I remember thinking, no one had ever looked at me before, that curiously.

"So you're Rosemary," he said. "You don't look too bad. I thought you'd be younger." He barely smiled, but his eyes lit up warmly.

"I thought you'd be older ... and I'm taller," I said triumphantly.

"Yeah," he said slowly, studying me sharply. "You're almost taller than the corn. Not me, I'm going to stay just this tall, so the corn's always higher and I can always walk through here, and no one can find me."

"I could find you! I could see your bright hair sticking out," I said jubilantly.

"Nah, I don't believe you." Peter said solemnly.

"Yes! Yes! I could see you from over there." I pointed to the little knoll of a hill where I had first seen the field.

"Nah, I don't think so," he said, with a twinkle in his eyes.

"I could too!" I protested, and Peter started to laugh. His eyes definitely started first and then his whole face. He laughed so hard, even his bright blond hair seemed to stand up and move with his laughter. And I started laughing too. We both went on for so long, we could hardly talk. We sat, surrounded by corn reaching up to the sky, laughing along with us.

"You're kinda silly, but for a girl, you're all right, Rosemary," Peter said, smiling up at the sun.

"You're okay too, Peter, for a boy, I mean, and a cousin," I said, giggling, as the breeze made the husks tickle my cheeks.

"Yeah, you're okay … It's gonna be okay that you're here, even though you are kinda funny looking, even though you are taller than the corn." Peter was laughing again.

"Yeah, well you're funny looking too, your hair looks brighter than the sun and your eyes are funny too, Peter! You know what, I think your eyes have wings … the way they turn up at the corners when you laugh, is so funny, and they kind of shine out and up to the sky, like wings ready to fly!" I was laughing again.

"Well, maybe I'm an angel, that's what my Gramma says … that's why I probably have wings … that's why I have freckles too." Peter laughed uproariously. "Every freckle is an angel's kiss, Gramma always says."

Now I was really impressed. I stopped laughing and stared at the freckled kisses and at the wings in Peter's eyes. "Friends?" I asked solemnly.

"Yeah, friends," Peter said, equally solemnly. And as we shook childish hands in the bright yellow cornfield on that golden day, the wings in Peter's eyes looked at me and smiled all the way up to the sky. I remember thinking then, maybe summer on the farm wouldn't be so bad.

My first summer away from the city turned out to be a summer of golden moments. It was a very full season, a time that gave me so many things. It gave me kites on sunny, breezy days and gardens of perfect flowers, my very own job picking blueberries and strawberries, my first relationships with animals and all living things. I began to know bees and ants and chickens and pigs. I developed a strong relationship with a friendly cow with soft brown eyes I called Nancy (after a girl from my school back home who also had brown eyes, and was called Nancy). The summer gave me clean fresh air to run in, more trees than I ever dreamed possible to climb, and best of all, the summer gave me a pal called Peter.

Peter and I became best of friends. He introduced me to and taught me all about farm life. He taught me a love for the country I have never let go of. It was the best summer of my life.

When we had to go back to New York in September, I thought I would die. As we drove away, my eyes were wet, even though Peter and I laughed. As we waved good-bye, the last thing I remember seeing were the tears in Peter's liquid, smiling eyes, flying further and further away.

Back home, in the fall and the winter, I counted the days until summer and realized more and more how much I missed the farm. I thought it was strange, though, that I now loved home and the city less. I wondered why, then, that love seemed to go away to different places and not come back home.

The following summer, I was ten and we were only able to spend one month on the farm for our vacation. Peter and I stepped back into our old routines and it was like we had never been separated. Our first summer together had never really ended and would go on forever again.

We wrote letters the following winter, and I began to know that Peter would always be a part of my life.

The next four summers followed the same pattern and even though we were both growing up fast, we remained the best of friends. Peter played so many roles for me, the brother I never had, a dad I could talk to, and a flirtatious, first boyfriend, teasing me, admiring me and always liking me, growing together in wisdom, understanding, wanting to hold on to our childish games, perhaps wanting to hold on to the innocence of life on the farm. But life was moving too fast and high school was upon us. I had other close friends at school but I knew it was the same for Peter as it was for me; there was a special bond between us and I knew that no one else would ever fill the place Peter filled in my life.

The summer I was fifteen, we had many long talks about our lives, what we would both do in the years ahead. Peter looked forward to college. He was extremely smart and I remember I said to him, "I can't believe you could ever leave here, ever leave this farm. If I were you, I would stay here forever."

Peter looked so far away when he answered me. "A part of me will always be here with this land but there's so much to learn, so much to do. I don't want to, but I have to go away for a while. I have to learn how we can keep this place going and I want to learn how to help other farmers make a better living too. Times are changing, Rosemary, farms are changing; the future here doesn't look good now. I have to learn and find ways to change that, and I will."

Peter was a rare and wonderful person: I had learned that through our summers together and through the years, I learned it more and more. He was so dedicated to helping other farmers, someday. I knew he would do it. He had such an aura about him and he still had the brightest eyes I'd ever seen in my life, eyes filled with a caring light that seemed to reach out to the world. Peter was a dreamer and a loner, so deeply caring, so sympathetic to the world, so sensitive, that sometimes I wanted to reach out and protect him. I wished then, he would stay with the cornfields he loved. I wondered what the world would do to him.

Peter turned his caring gaze on me then, looking at me so sharply, trying hard to plow a path through my mind and into my heart. "And you, Rosemary, what will you do? Why don't you get out of that stinking city and come out here ... you could go to school out here."

"I wish I could, Peter, but you know how much it means to my father for me to go to school back East and then step right into his business. I can even work part-time with him while I go to school, like he's always wanted me to."

"Is that what you want, Rosemary?" Peter looked doubtful.

"Yes, of course," I smiled. I knew if I said it enough, eventually I would believe it.

I wished that beautiful month together would never end, a month when I was almost sixteen and still filled with hope, and still believed that some things would never end, the world would always go on, and everything would always be all right.

The day before my trip back to New York, Peter and I walked through the cornfields. Peter stopped suddenly and looked at me so intently. He always had such a look, so curious, so intent on knowing everything, seeing everything, being touched by everything in the world, eyes that seemed to fly everywhere, taking everything in.

He said, "Rosemary, promise me you won't change, you'll never stop laughing, hoping."

As I looked at his face, I knew he wouldn't take any promise lightly; he wanted me to think deeply about what I said. I looked at the corn and the sun and then at him. "I will never stop hoping, laughing ... if you won't."

"I promise," he said solemnly.

"Will we always be friends, Peter?"

"Always, Rosemary." And he took my hand and we walked slowly out of a golden cornfield and into different worlds.

In the years through college and after, we never lost touch, though there were no more summers on the farm. We wrote once in a while, and called. There were very occasional weekends together and the summer after I graduated from college, Peter flew up to New York to see me. I showed him the city, and he seemed so proud of me when I showed him my new office in the business my father owned part of.

I laughed as I said, "Someday this will all be mine."

I remember, Peter didn't laugh; he looked at me so carefully and said only, "Do you want this all to be yours, Rosemary?"

"Of course," I laughed lightly but his steady gaze made me feel sad. I wasn't sure just why.

It was so good to see Peter; he always made me feel that just when the world is dry, when there's nothing left to drink, he would be there bearing a very pure water. He always made me feel stronger, made me feel like anything was possible, that life was possible.

He had a light about him, a light that radiated out of his eyes and said, "We can save ourselves; we can save the world."

He talked about his life and it sounded so full. He was doing so much work, trying to help farmers. He was working twelve hours a day.

"Mom's worried about losing our place, since Dad died ... but I won't let it happen! I will never let that happen, Rosemary."

Something about the way he said it worried me, made me wonder if the fight was going to be too much. But he didn't say anymore. There was just one moment when his eyes looked hurt, so hurt, I knew that the battle had already been fierce. I put my hand on his head, running my fingers through his thick blond locks. I wanted to comfort him, I wanted to say something, anything, but I didn't. Peter was my angel and yes, perhaps the world's angel too. But angels were strong; he didn't need me. I needed him.

We talked about how quickly I would move up in the company, how wonderful my life would be in the city. We talked about spending a few weeks together, in the spring on the farm. And then he left, flew back to his world, a world that needed him more than I did, or at least thought so.

My office, my life, was darker without Peter, filled with the quiet of a missing light.

We never did get together that spring. I couldn't get away from my job and Peter was busy too. He longed to spend the summer on the farm, but he too was busy, trying to fight his world.

When I received the letter telling me his mother had died, I cried, thinking about my Aunt Helen. I wished I hadn't been in Europe on business, I know I would have gone to the farm.

I thought of my mother and how she had loved Helen, and I cried once more, tears my mother would have cried if she were alive. I tried to call Peter but I couldn't reach him. I knew how alone he must have felt. My parents were both gone now and I knew how that made me feel. I knew that Bobby Jr. was in the army and no one knew where Henry was these days, and I worried some more about Peter and then I relaxed; Peter would be all right, Peter was always all right. And then life went on, or should I say, a reasonable facsimile passed by.

Years went by, and moments, days when Peter tried to call me but I was away on business. He sent me a postcard from California and I wrote him a letter. I tried to call. So many unconnected lines.

He called, one afternoon in June last year, just days after I had been given the position of Vice President of the company. I was so happy to hear from him I cried.

"Peter! What are you up to? I miss you so much! I haven't heard from you in so long! Where are you?"

"I'm back here in the heartland of America ... only, Rosemary, I don't think there's any heart left here." He laughed quietly.

"Oh, Peter, it's so good to hear your voice; I have so much to tell you! I'm the new V.P., as of this week!"

"I'm so proud of you. You're all right, Rosemary, for a girl anyway."

I laughed so hard, I don't think I heard any of the pain in Peter's laughter. "When will I see you? When can you come up here?"

"I don't know, Rosemary."

"You have to come soon, Peter ... I can't stand it ... it's been too, too long! I think of you all the time."

"I think of you too … part of me is there with you, Rosemary, always."

"I know it, Peter, you're my guardian angel." I breathed softly, trying to stifle a sob.

"Well close your eyes and maybe you'll feel my wings, or better yet, the kiss of an angel. Goodnight, Rosemary. I never told you this before, but you're my angel too!"

Before I could say another word, he hung up, our line disconnected, words ended, feelings left over. I listened to the cold hum for a moment, hoping Peter would come back, and slowly, reluctantly, I put the phone down and away.

Peter's angel? No, I couldn't be anyone's angel; I didn't have wings. "Peter was the one with the wings," I smiled. "If I could be anyone's angel, though, I wish it would be Peter's," I thought sadly.

Time moves so slowly when you don't know how to fly. The next year was a difficult one. My new position brought me more worries and new frustrations. Somehow I missed summer, that year. It passed by my office window but I never saw it. I wasn't looking out at the time.

Winter, that year, I didn't want to see, and spring, I vowed I would find but I never had the time. This summer would be different, though. This would at last be my summer. I would finally take some time off. I would get in touch with Peter, force him to take time off, and we would take a vacation, go back to the farm. Yes, we would walk through cornfields and relax and laugh again.

Late in May, I stood up to close our annual business meeting and I looked casually around the gray board room. Something made me stop and glance slowly around the room. I looked at every worried face and in every dingy corner, and such a strange feeling came over me. I wanted so much to find something in that room. On that day, I felt I had to find it, right then. But it was missing completely.

I knew it then, finally, without a single doubt, it just wasn't there.

There was no spirit left in the room, no life in the company, not a spark in one pale face, not a light in anyone's eyes. I saw it all at once, there was no life. The very full room of tired men and women had all turned off their lights, had all taken off their wings, discarded them absently; they were too cumbersome for the world.

In a society that seemed to require two feet on the ground, wings were no longer necessary and they were broken far too easily. If they weren't taken off slowly, gradually, while one wasn't looking, while one didn't care, the world would rip them off at some point and that would hurt, the pain would be too much. And for most, it was a very numbing pain. But for some, the pain was so sharp that they could never stop, never stop screaming.

I went back to my dark office, and sat at my tired desk. I looked down at my hands and found that they were unmoving, so motionless, too deadened to care what they held in their grasp, no feeling left in the fingertips. I wondered when the ice of the world had put them to sleep.

I looked at my face in the mirror, the steadiness of my gaze made me wonder if there was still some light there or only a vacant lie. Did the fixation of my eyes cause the light not to move, remain hidden, or had it drifted into some dream, only to be gone forever.

I thought of Peter and I was afraid. And then I remembered. I too had wings long ago, small ones perhaps, but wings nonetheless. I never saw, I never knew they had to be nurtured, guarded, treasured. I thought they were some casual playthings that would be there when I wanted them, waiting for me patiently to join them for the afternoon, for the summer, unobtrusively in the background, ready at all times, within reach, when I was in the mood for them, when I wanted them, when I needed them too desperately. And they came in their package, brand new, in excellent condition, never needing any care, any cleaning, any polishing, their shine would remain through my life, preserved by some kind God.

But that was not what I saw in my mirror. I saw shriveled stumps I'd forgotten how to use, unused wings that

I'd forgotten how to maneuver, wings that had begun to disintegrate, like leaves of yellowed books, moth-eaten horrors that had begun to evaporate into the timelessness that had so graciously given them to me, an immaculate magical gift that I had found so easy to lose, to throw back in the face of some patient, knowing God. How had I dared!

I left my company that day, on a leave of absence, to find what was really absent from my life. I spent three weeks sitting in my home on the fifteenth floor, searching in corners. I looked out of my living room window at the street below. I saw people whose spirits were dying. They walked quickly, trailing liquid wings that slowly melted into the ground, unseen by dazed eyes that hurried through their motion-filled worlds. I wondered how many things had dissolved into the Earth along with their wings; dreams, innocence, caring, even puddles of love, rusting alone in the gutters, hope that had turned blood-red as it dripped slowly out of forgotten dreams.

I walked to my old mirror and peered into its frozen depths. "Rosemary old girl, what have you become, who are you now," I said slowly, carefully, to only myself, as I stared into the glass. There was no answer. I felt unsure, defeated by my unknowingness, my strength sapped by a hazy depression. I spent day after night aimlessly wondering, drifting around the corners of the home where the shell called Rosemary pretended to live.

And then, one quiet morning, I woke up from a dream. In it I had seen a place I remembered from long ago, a place that reminded me of heaven, a heaven where angels flew through golden skies, riding on puffy white clouds filled with hope.

I got up out of bed to look out of a bedroom window where rays of light streamed down to me from a strong, yellow sun. I knew then that there was still some light left in the world for me. I was like a prisoner who had committed a terrible crime and was confined without food or water. My world was dry, so very dry. But on that sunlit morning, I knew there was still some water left in the world for me. I made the first promise of my life that I really understood. I looked again in the dark, gilded, hall mirror and I promised myself to find any drops of liquid still left.

I was happier after that. I felt filled with purpose. I knew I wanted to change my life and I began to. I decided a long vacation on the farm would be just what the doctor ordered. I also longed for some really pure water to drink. I called Peter.

Every call I made led to another dead end. Peter seemed to be unreachable. It made me think long and hard about how we had lost touch. I knew I had never forgotten Peter but I wondered when I had stopped really looking at him. I had allowed that angel to fly out of my life slowly and now he was missing, had disappeared behind some cloud, in a world that had become foreign to me.

But I went on with my plans. I would leave in a few weeks for Indiana and by then, Peter and I would connect.

I was looking forward to a very different summer when the call came, on that warm Saturday in June; a call made, received and ending a lifetime of disconnected lines. The wires would never again be alive with a sensitive spirit called Peter. And the opportunity to transmit my life through those wires to him was gone forever, taken away from me.

What savage beast or uncaring butterfly had broken Peter's wings and removed him from my world? What sad fate searches out innocent promises? Who are the demons that burn down our houses of laughter and of hope?

It would be the hardest thing I would ever do now, to go to the funeral home. It would be so hard to face those eyes for the last time. And there was no longer any farm to run back to. I don't know why, but I thought of the bowl of strawberries swimming through the thick cream I had tasted on my first visit to the farm. I saw visions of Peter running through the cornfields and I was afraid, afraid for myself, and afraid for the world. Would there ever be berries and corn again? Who would be left to grow them?

I packed my bags and walked slowly away from my world. I waited on the cold street for the cab to come that would start me on my journey to Indiana. I stood amidst the crashing noise of lifeless spirits and surveyed the farmlands of New York City. Would I ever look down from my window on the fifteenth floor and see strawberries growing through the iron clad concrete? No, there would be no luscious berries ever growing on those dirty streets.

As the driver threw my bags quickly into the smoky cab, I had another question on my mind. How much time was left? How long would corn dance and grow and wait for us, untended in golden fields? Would farms continue to disappear into the brittle cold, lifeless ground, taking with them the spirits of the few that still carried their wings, proudly for all to see?

I remembered what had once shown from Peter's eyes, what I would never see again. In one moment and thirty-five quick years, my world had turned to a bitter dryness. Peter was gone! I could never go back and change our past but I would start now to be Peter's angel, too late for Peter, but maybe someday, not too late for the world. I had half a wing left and the other wing would mend in Indiana. I jumped into the cab and I knew I would never look back.

32

PASSION AND THE COURAGE TO FLY

The Wings Of His Eyes ended and I felt as though I had been dropped from the center of a cyclone into the middle of a golden cornfield, where I felt like hiding amongst the yellow ears of corn and mending my bruised spirit. When I looked up from my typewriter, the cornfield had quickly become my room but my need to mend remained. Though this story had ended in a strong, positive place, I rode on a roller coaster of emotions to get there.

Just prior to beginning this story, I had been meeting Rosemary in my dream journeys. I don't know if she was really aware of me or if she thought I was part of her dreams. I wondered if maybe her desire to express these powerful feelings had somehow attracted me to her moment in time. I felt her unconscious permission to merge with her emotions and senses and experience this story through her.

It's difficult to explain this process that I experience, this merging with another person in such a completely emotional and sensory manner. I could see and feel events through her senses, her eyes and ears and taste and touch. And yet I could also feel her emotions as she felt them, and even feel her values and inner decision making processes. At times I felt as though I was actually her and yet, there was always my sense of self just off to the side, quietly witnessing, never intruding, always amazed.

As I finished this story, I completely understood why it had been necessary to prepare me emotionally for this experience. Merging with Rosemary in the beginning of this story was like stepping into a raging river of emotion. I saw my first glimpse of her world through the salty, distorted sting of tears rushing up and out in a flood of horror and confusion. I felt the texture of her world with hands that shook like leaves in a storm, trembling and quaking in the wake of some vast unseen force. I felt her world become suddenly strange and unfamiliar, losing its safe sameness and its distance. As time seemed to grind to a halt, I could see her world become all too present and much too clear.

The world of the present had stopped abruptly, had ended its dizzying pace, losing whatever mysterious power that had pushed it on and on. Rosemary was just beginning to discover that it wasn't her heart that moved her world of business and meetings, her endless comings and goings. A feeling of discontentment and doubt had already begun to stir in her. A sense of emptiness and a look of despair had glanced back at her from the mirror, exposing to her the lie that her life had become. Rosemary was confused and faltering on her once steady track, when the call came and everything stopped. I could feel her emotions step in, bringing healing and wholeness to her.

There was a river of feeling that carried Rosemary back to the farm of her childhood and the summer of her very first visit. I was amazed at how vivid her memories were. I felt myself on those currents of feeling and memory, moving into her past as if it were my own. I felt her little girl feelings and fears, her innocent joys and wonders. During those passages, as I typed and listened, I felt like a child again. This process of merging with another was taking me to places and into experiences in which my own personal boundaries and identity could evaporate, if only for a moment. The feeling could be, at the same time, delightful, exhilarating and deeply unsettling.

I saw Rosemary from inside her life, from the inside of her experiences. I felt her decisions and choices, and what moved those choices, and I became, at times, confused. I think that the most confusing times, for me, were the years at the law firm, her father's firm. As she told me that chapter of her story, I could sense the loss of feeling in her, I could feel it fade away, as though Rosemary was losing her ability to dream and losing her sense of self.

There was no heart in this life that she had worked and studied so hard to make. She felt, to me at times, like a train, moving powerfully and purposely down a long, difficult track. But increasingly I could feel that it wasn't her track, it was a way laid down for her by a loving, well-meaning father who simply wanted to pass on to her his accomplishments and opportunities. It had always been assumed that she would take over and "of course" she would. Rosemary had to put her feelings aside in order to stay on that track, had to fold her wings and simply persevere. I could feel her drying up inside as she forced herself on and on.

The morning after I finished Rosemary's story, Rick got his first chance to see what I had been working on for two weeks. I woke up early, placed the typewritten copy on his night table, tip toed quietly out of the room and into the kitchen to put on our morning coffee. I put on my robe, grabbed a cup of the steaming brew and stepped out on to the balcony of our third floor apartment. The morning was cold and still, and the coffee cup steamed higher in protest as I drew the robe's soft collar closer to my throat. I stood for a moment and started to reach back for the handle on the sliding glass door, when something stopped me, called to me quietly from the woods nearby.

I stepped back, away from the door and towards the gray, wooden, frost covered railing where my gaze became fixed on the tree-tops. Birds by the hundreds decorated the stark limbs of the trees, like glistening, shivering ornaments. They flitted from place to place, their sounds sputtering and bubbling in the crisp morning air. Suddenly a long piercing cry cut through the growing din of tiny bird sounds. The gathering crowds of birds seemed to settle down as though called to attention. The cry peeled again like a pure bell ringing, calling flocks of worshipers to their prayers. I held my breath and looked up at the single tree that rose sharply up near the balcony and shot right past it even further into the sky. At the top, a huge solitary hawk perched and surveyed his kingdom. His long calls brought

RICK & LOUISA CLERICI

a kind of order and peace to those shimmering cold moments.

All fell silent as time stood reverently still. I could feel one of my guides come close to me. She too was speechless, joining me simply to share in the wordless beauty of this world. I could feel her absolute respect for the universe and all its beings, and her joy in being a part of it all.

I felt blessed to have stepped out and into this magical scene. I turned and went in with the hopes of rousing Rick and coaxing him out to share the few remaining moments of this beautiful morning. I found him sitting up in bed, story in hand and a solitary tear softly moving down his cheek. He looked up at me without words for his feelings and stretched out his arms to hold me. We both cried as we held each other, cried for the beauty, the sadness, the lost wings, the feeling of life and living that sometimes only tears can express.

Over morning breakfast, having regained our composure somewhat, we talked on and on about Rosemary and Peter. Rick felt deeply moved by their story and by the issues it raised. Rick said, "I can see more than ever how incredibly important it is that we stay in touch with our feelings. Our emotions give us access to that level of information that is essential, like dreams, desires, the sacredness of all life, the messages of nature and our ties to the land."

"I could feel Rosemary's emotions, they were very real and strong," I recalled, "but there was something that seemed to over ride her emotions and take precedence. I think it was her sense of duty, her duty to her father and her family."

"Absolutely," Rick agreed, and added, "I think her life in the city may also have added to her loss of feeling. Cities are magical places, but they're all about people magic ... and people are only part of the whole. Remember what you told me about the hawk, this morning, how wondrous and wordless that experience was for you? People magic can become so full of itself and words and intellect. It can become so very lost."

I could feel the tears come when I talked about Peter. "I think you're right ... Peter's life on the farm kept him closer to nature and to his own nature. In Peter's world, people lived in harmony with nature ... depended on nature ... really had to respect what was natural."

Rick chimed in, "And in Rosemary's world, most of nature had been eradicated to make room for business and people. What remained of nature, like parks, was neatly enclosed and contained. And Rosemary could do that too, she could contain what was natural in her, she could remove herself from the messiness and turbulence of feelings."

I thought about what Rick had said. "I guess Peter's death was like an earthquake that even the city couldn't contain or keep out. I really felt Rosemary change after Peter's death. I think she found something in herself that she thought had died, long ago. I think she found her wings."

We talked on like this for hours. It was a part of this journey of storytelling that I loved dearly, this flow of sharing of ideas and feelings that became an important part of our lives together. The stories helped to make our wings grow stronger and helped us dare to fly

33

BANGING ON THE DOORS OF MY TRANCE

I remember the night clearly. It was early on a Friday evening in March. The temperature had hit nearly sixty degrees in the afternoon and at seven o'clock was still in the mid fifties. It was an inordinately warm day for March in Massachusetts and to New Englanders desperate for spring, it felt like eighty. I was daydreaming in the office of our apartment. The breeze curled in through the window that I was reluctant to close. The light was very dim; somehow my reluctance also covered turning on the lamp.

I mused in the early evening darkness, almost oblivious to the passage of time, when a noise outside quickly caught my attention. There was a jostling murmur of human sounds that gradually became discernible as voices and their accompanying bodies. I listened for a while before I recognized the sound of teenagers, preparing to party in the nearby woods. They swarmed about with military-like intent, carrying cases of beer and liquor hoisted on shoulders, in single file like columns of ants.

The noise died down, faded into the background for a time, and in that time, I drifted back and deeper into my reverie. I began to feel the silent presence of my spirit guides in the room.

Perhaps I should try to describe the experience of becoming aware of my guides. Often, in these moments of musing and drifting, I feel my thinking and feeling process expanding. I sense my attention reaching, in a playful dream-like way, into deeper levels of awareness, reaching for another point of view. As my awareness expands, I sense the approach of another awareness in the process of expanding. Like two beautiful bubbles, these awarenesses drift towards each other, often merging and sharing view points, information and energy. As these bubbles of awareness approach, I can feel those that are familiar to me, by their vibrations, their subtle signatures of identity. Given a few moments, I always recognize my guides and welcome them. Our meeting always requires our mutual consent.

In the midst of this wordless sharing of awareness, I began to sense, once again, the energy of the partying teenagers in the woods. Their energy came careening through the window and banged on the doors of my trance. Their vibrations were intrusive and angry and the level of their hostility rose with the increase in their drunkenness. I began to draw back a bit from my trance, only to hear the screaming and swearing that was getting louder by the minute. I could also hear what sounded like the breaking of bottles against rocks and trees and the constant throwing of beer cans.

Slowly, at first, the anger in me began to build. It angered me deeply to think of these careless people indiscriminately trampling over plants, injuring trees, and throwing their trash in the woods.

At the same time and much to my surprise, I could sense my guides as they seemed to fill with disgust. I'm not sure that I've ever felt the deep anger and almost rage that I could sense from my guides. It's difficult to describe their emotions and the way those emotions are expressed. It seems as though their feelings, rather than forming and changing from one emotion to another in a linear way, are layered one upon another, occurring simultaneously. The anger that I sensed was mixed with sorrow and awareness, like a wave of rage moving through an ocean of wisdom and sadness.

Finally my guides simply said, "We could write about this." Their emotions always seem to move them to respond creatively.

A week later, on a rainy cold night, a story began coming through. Just before the story began, I heard these words, very clearly. "We come to you in your words, the translation having been made in another world." This curious statement set the tone for the rest of this strange story. Though it took me three weeks and many nights to finish, I was fascinated from the very first sentence.

What language this story was translated from, I'm not sure, but most probably it would be spoken *In The Light of Another Moon.*

34

IN THE LIGHT OF ANOTHER MOON

I woke up from a very deep sleep too early, again, too early. I felt concerned; was I losing control in some way? Even perhaps, losing power? "No! Do not even begin to create these words, Kirin ... don't do this," I told myself.

Just to be sure, I looked out of the hole, slowly lifting my head to the sky and then down again quickly. It was true, I saw not believing, the sixth moon was just beginning to rise in the western sky. I had never been awake on the planet this early. I returned back into the resting place, as far into the hole as I could go. I thought I was safe, but then I caught a glimpse of myself in the "seeing glass" and I started to scream over and over and over. "No! No! No!"

Danal couldn't sleep. He sat in this hole of unrest that had been arranged for him and slowly turned the night's events over in his mind. He didn't like what had happened at all, being forced to land on this foreign planet. No, it had not been the plan at all and he was becoming increasingly uneasy. He was beginning to think this planet was a very strange place and not to his liking. A thick feeling of some compelling unease seemed to float in the air, beckoning him, trying to softly alert him.

He had, of course, heard much about this planet. Much was not a surprise. But to really be here, marooned in this eerie hole, this "resting place," unable to move about the planet freely, waiting for some seventh moon to appear, unable to go and speak to his partner of this horrible journey, the only other survivor of his ship. Danal wondered if he too was probably awake, in whatever small hole they had put him in. This is horrible, he thought, I cannot rest!

———•———

Dr. Meca sat in his own place of rest, wondering what was next, wondering where they had put Danal. Was he too stuck in one of these miserable holes? And why am I so afraid; what is this uneasiness I feel? The lack of sound ... Then he realized, with a start, there is no sound! My God, there is no sound! I could be the only life breathing on this planet. He stopped his thoughts, motionless, trying not to hear his breath, disbelieving at first, and then knowing. No sound existed, a sickening knowing. My God, it's almost as if, no, it's ... it's like all life stops during their nights, nights of rotating moons. He shuddered hard and then began to pace back and forth in the small space. And then needing, needing so to hear the sound of his own voice, he started to speak out loud, speaking to an empty hole.

"It must be some trick, some effect they create. From the little I've seen, their world does seem filled with effects. It's probably not unusual, they probably find it soothing. Yes, I know, I'm surrounded by life of all kinds, here in the middle of their largest city, and we know this planet is filled with life. Nothing to feel strange about." Meca breathed a calming sigh and kept on speaking even louder.

"Let's see, we know this is a highly civilized planet, one of the oldest in this galaxy, some believe perhaps one of the oldest in the history of life. They have a long and colorful past. Many systems of government and rebellion have juggled places. In the year 5072, a system was created called the Gayan Eye. I know I've heard some say that the Gayan Eye had never before existed in the history of planetary civilization. Travelers that journeyed here to this lonely outpost brought back some stories, curious tales, but the too few travelers did not bring back enough information for us to really know the truth. In the century since, I have heard some say that the Gayan Eye was the fairest rule of any planet ever known. 'Perhaps too fair,' others said."

I was beginning to feel more relaxed already, watching my own thoughts work. "No need to get excited, this is a highly refined place."

"As far as I know, the Gayan Eye is a system of rules, behavior and government. Every citizen of the planet has, what they call, an opening, and then an ongoing life relationship with this eye, open to the rule of the land, so to speak. Even visitors must go through this opening ... no, that's only a fearful rumor ... I think." I shuddered, and in that very moment as I trembled, a strange orange light came through the hole, throwing a darkly thick orange glow on everything in sight. The thought came into my head that the planet had finally awakened. And then I heard a noise from somewhere outside, it sounded like a very long sigh.

Danal peered out of his hole, just as two very tall men peered in.

"You will come with us," they said, in one toneless voice in unison, reaching in to take his hand.

Danal gave them his hand readily; he had been waiting for this, knew it was coming. He tried to think clearly.

"Why, where do you take me?"

"To connect with the High Minister," they said, disinterestedly, in unison, pulling him into a tiny boat.

"Where is my partner, Meca?" He tried to sound calm.

"He connects also." The pair turned their eyes away from him, gazing only at the small white boat they guided through the dark orange waters.

Danal turned his attention to the scenery. It looked much worse now than when they had landed. I think the light from this seventh moon is too bright, he thought uneasily.

Danal entered the large, ominous room at the very same time he saw Meca enter from the opening on the other side. He wondered if this was going to be a casual meeting of friends or a ceremony between aliens. Their eyes met for one brief instant, trying to reassure each other. Danal saw Meca's curiosity mixed with fear and Meca saw Danal's fear mixed with curiosity.

Then a woman stepped from a high, white platform and came towards them slowly, each of her careful steps measured. She seemed to be measuring the two of them. With both long arms outstretched towards them, the odd, white palms of her hands facing them, she simply smiled.

"Join in awareness," she whispered solemnly, touching Danal's fingertips lightly and then Meca's.

"Join in awareness," they answered in unison. Meca smiled as he wondered if she would be pleased that they knew the traditional greeting of this orange planet.

"Welcome to Theorin. Please be with ease," she said, as three seats came up through the floor, almost as if they knew just where the three would stand, exactly.

As the tall woman sat first into the shiny, white chair, her fingertips stayed in the same position, facing Danal, watching Meca.

"I am the one called Kirin, High Minister of zone 94. I am in happiness to greet you. I wish you the brightest awareness in your stay with us. We understand the ending, the crashing of your ship, and we connect and welcome you. May your stay be as long as you wish, and fruitful. We wish, too, to know more of your people."

"Why did your help not come sooner, when we landed?" Meca had to know, hear something, some reason.

"You arrive during the fifth moon, when all is in the resting place; only few are able to come to you then."

"Is that why we were taken immediately into ... into those holes?" Meca was feeling braver.

"No one sees the light of the six moons; we were extending to you our privilege to be at rest during the six lights. We will give you refreshment and then you will have time to explore the city, if you wish, before the first moon comes. Then you will return to your resting places. When the seventh moon comes again, the tribunal will meet and we will speak again. Until then, we allow you to share our practice of the six moons."

But she did not tell us what murky delights we would not see. As we were led out, she only said, "Remember, there is no rest before the first moon."

Later, we would look back on this first meeting and realize that when High Minister Kirin said "remember," she thought we knew.

We walked slowly into the city, only exchanging looks, afraid to voice our thoughts. I know I had a feeling of fear and a feeling of heaviness, as if the rust-colored mist surrounding us was pressing against us, pushing against our shoulders, weighing us down. I think Meca felt this too.

"Good Doctor, what are your thoughts in this situation?" I asked, finally, in fear.

"I feel oddly uneasy, with no real reason." he hesitated, "I guess they seem welcoming enough, though this tribunal makes me wonder. I don't know, Danal, and this orange gaseous substance ... what is it anyway? It's everywhere, it even covers their streets." Meca looked a little pale. "It seems harmless enough ... it's like the blue gases in the atmosphere of Cirrus. But you're right, this bothers me more too, though maybe because there really isn't anything that looks orange back home ... maybe it's that simple ... we're not used to it. I wish we had instruments on the ship to measure it ... God, I wish we had a ship left, I'd get out of here ... this whole place makes me feel strange."

We continued walking through the city, a city of pearly white structures, surrounded by orange dust. The air held the thick, reddish-yellow light of the seventh moon, now high in the sky, hovering over us expectantly.

There were few beings on the streets, only a small mixture from different worlds, none of whom seemed interested in speaking with us.

"They seem like very quiet people, Meca, don't they ... very calm," I remarked.

"No, they are not calm ... I don't know what they are, but it is not calm."

"Are they not free perhaps? Some tyranny here, we don't see?" My eyes searched the empty street in front of us.

"That is exactly the feeling, Danal, but they appear free. They live, they work, they walk in this city, appearing free ... all looks free ... and yet ...? They seem closed in some way, or preoccupied, totally and completely preoccupied. I wish we knew what happens during their nights."

"Nothing happens. They rest, Meca, in their holes."

"No, something happens, I'm almost sure of it ... and we have to find out what it is, Danal."

"I'm more interested in what's going to happen to us, during that tribunal. You know some of the old stories about this place, Meca. You've heard them too."

"That's why we have to know them, find out what's going on here so we're prepared. Let's meet here by those gates, Danal. During the resting time, we'll sneak out of those holes and meet here."

"I don't know, it feels too dangerous ... besides, they seem to be treating us as friends ... I don't know."

All of a sudden, my words were cut off by a loud, screeching sound. Stunned, my whole body shook with fear as I looked at Meca. Then there was a great movement in the city. Beings from all directions came out of buildings, and moved quickly down the streets towards their resting holes. Meca and I looked to the sky, as the seventh moon descended towards the ground, its orange light fading into the dust.

"Let's go!" Meca grabbed my shaking arm and we ran together as more and more sirens lit up a tumultuous city. The sound was deafening and we ran with our heads down, trying to escape from the noise, holding our ears tightly. When we got to my hole, Meca practically pushed me inside with fear.

"Remember, meet me ... wait for the second moon," and he became a blur in the hurrying crowd. I dropped into the hole, completely out of breath, crawling as far in as I could, filled with a feeling that I would never dare to leave this resting place.

———•———

Meca paced and paced, looking out periodically, oh so briefly peering at the sky. How long is it between these moons, he thought? He felt impatient, wanting to get this over with.

"The tension in here feels like a prison cell, not a resting place," he yelled, at no one in particular. There was no one there.

He began to picture the planet, how many holes there must be, and how many beings were hiding in those holes. Hiding from what? Then he realized this wouldn't do, he would have to relax, keep calm, if he was going to do what he must do. He took a deep breath and looked quietly out of the hole. The second moon was beginning to rise. He hesitated for a moment and looked around the tiny, dim room. Then he steadied himself and leaped from the hole and with a feeling of freedom, he started running in the dark of a quiet, lifeless planet.

Meca crouched in back of the gate, waiting silently in the dark, his cold body motionless, his mind racing with fear, tension and something called curiosity. He had seen nothing, no one. All was darkness, quietness. The city looked empty, not a sound coming from anywhere. And where was Danal? The second moon was already fading from view. What should he do if Danal didn't get here? He climbed slowly and quietly on some rocks behind the gate and looked in the direction of Danal's hole. He saw no movement. The air was stiff and heavy, unbending. He turned slowly in each direction, not a sound anywhere. And then, all of a sudden, he thought he saw a flash of light. He stopped, his eyes straining to see through the gloomy air. He saw nothing, at first, and then there it was again! Another flash, coming from a distant part of the city. Meca looked around once more, his eyes pleading to see Danal.

Then he climbed down the rocks, filled with a cold fear and a deep hunger to know. As the third moon rose silently in the sky, he pulled his right foot forward and all of a sudden he was off, facing towards a flash in the night.

———•———

Kirin sighed and leaned back into the softness of her white chair. She watched the golden liquid sizzle and bubble in the tall goblet she held with both hands. Taking a long sip, she allowed the sweet sharpness of the velvety liquid to drift slowly down her throat. Aah, it tasted good. She felt tired, there had been so much work, so many beings arriving on the planet. She thought of the last two who had crashed their ship and she felt a little uneasy. They seemed different. They seemed to know of Theorin, its customs, and yet they seemed unafraid. She wondered who they really were. Oh well, she would find out all about them tomorrow. "The seventh moon will be upon us soon enough, and tonight, I'm tired. I will sleep well!"

She took off the white, silky band from her forehead, and was ready to give herself to the Gods of sleep but her eye was drawn to the Seeing Glass. She smiled at her own curiosity, "Don't be silly, Kirin, go to sleep, forget those two, they're just warriors from a primitive planet, nothing unusual ... the doctor, perhaps a little more curious than most."

She turned away from the glass but then back, it seemed to be glowing a little bit brighter, almost like it was trying to get her attention, attract her back to the Seeing Glass. And Kirin did turn back toward it and as if speaking to it, said, "Well, one quick look ..." And her pale fingers touched the smoothness of the glass. But she was not prepared for what she saw. The picture was of Meca, running quickly in the darkness outside.

"What is he doing!" she screamed with fury, then she raced out of the hole, hurrying towards the vision in her glass.

———•———

The flashing light seemed to get stronger as Meca approached. It came from a small, silvery-white tower on the outskirts of the city. Meca looked apprehensively towards the sky; time was running out, he worried. He had to be back in the hole where they would find him in the morning. Should he go back now? He couldn't shake the feeling that someone, something was watching him, some alert quietness. But there was only a steely silence guarding the secrets of this planet. He kept moving, he had to know. He walked stealthily towards the entrance. A low hum seemed to be emitting from the structure. The only thing alive now, on the planet, was here, Meca thought.

As he got close to the entrance, he saw the pointed bars. They seemed to be emitting an orange light and they were the source of the staticy noise he had been hearing. There was no way in here. It was obviously an alarm of some kind, too dangerous. He had to find another way. But as he circled the tomb-like structure, he saw no other opening.

Then with a quick idea, he climbed slowly to the top of the cliff on the north side of the tower. From here, he could clearly see the three holes where a dim light flashed constantly, at regular intervals, quietly flashing over the planet. But it was not quiet. Now that he was on the other side of the building, the hum of the alarm had faded a little and he realized there was another noise, a strange muffled sound, coming from deep inside the tower.

"If there was only some way to climb into those light holes," Meca worried. And time was running out, the sixth moon was high in the sky. He began to feel like a crazed animal and ran down the cliff towards the entrance. He stopped short, sharply, as he felt the heat from the glowing bars touch his face. He felt, all of a sudden, unable to move. It was as if the hum from the entrance alarm had taken over his body, holding him securely in place. He felt like he couldn't even think. He was paralyzed!

A woman's voice seemed to come from a long distance away, screaming at him. "What do you want here, Meca?"

He answered as if he was in slow motion, could hardly open his mouth, could barely speak. "I want ... to go ... inside ... the tower." He felt as if he was in a daze; he still couldn't move, but he didn't really want to.

And then, he was on the other side of the claw-like bars, inside the tower. The High Minister stood facing him angrily, holding a peculiar light to his eyes. Meca thought, "She's going to kill me!" He leaned against the wall for support.

Kirin only said, "You are here inside the Tower of Tuin." There was a terrible silence, no longer even a hum. A coldness seemed to float around him, creeping into his body, into his soul. Meca was too petrified to move, even breathe.

Then, all at once, the walls seemed to shudder with a horrible burst. There was a hellish noise, a sound of tormented creatures wailing and screaming, with their last breath. Crashing screams filled the room with a raw, powerful energy. Meca's fingers clawed into the metal wall behind him, in fear. The crying sounds were so loud, so torturous, he thought the tower would come down over him and Kirin. But Kirin didn't even move, didn't even blink, stood calmly facing him, looking deeply into his eyes.

He felt dizzy, all at once. A blackness seemed to creep over him. He felt as if he was slipping into some strange unconsciousness. And then he gave up the fight and let go, and went quickly into the welcoming silence.

———•+•———

Danal sat rigid in the chair, his eyes stuck open with sleeplessness. He knew the seventh moon was beginning to rise. He had spent the period of the six moons torturing himself, wondering if Meca had left his hole, worrying about him, thinking he should have gone too, thinking he shouldn't have gone, and was relieved he didn't, wanting to have gone, filled with new fears.

They would soon come to get him, he knew. The two men would come for him and place him in their purposeful boat. And where would they sail to now? What new journey would those orange waters carry him to? What tribunal would greet him and Meca, if Meca was alive? Perhaps Meca had never left his resting hole. Perhaps he had found everything we wanted to know. Danal was filled with a deep uneasiness, an uneasiness there was no way to see through.

He looked out of the resting hole, to see the light from the seventh moon drifting downward, to blend with an orange sea. He saw the two men in the white boat, sailing towards him, in the distance a fiery ocean on one side, and land colored with a rust-like mist, on the other side of the resting hole. It was such a murky world out there, he thought, sadly.

For one brief moment, Danal wished he could plunge into the water, and sink, unseen to the bottom of that riveting sea. He wondered what the orange floor would look like. Then, as he saw the two stone-faced men come towards him; he reached out to them, with his trembling hands.

———•———

The large assemblage contained beings from many different planets, from many different worlds, all gathered together in the high tower room, for some compelling event. Danal felt hundreds of eyes staring at him, as he entered the gleaming tower, hundreds of noses seemed to sense he had arrived. But no one spoke, not a word, nor a sound, or even a welcoming gesture, silence, complete and dead.

Danal felt fear rise up and tingle through his body, going straight into the cavity of his being. He was beginning to feel a confusing terror, a terror without explanation. But then he wondered, did terror need any reason, any sense for being? Perhaps it was more like an unusual flower that one happened upon occasionally in the world, a plant whose smell would stupefy one into a heightened state of painful sleep. He felt dazed with the terror growing in the room. Danal was led to his seat, all the while searching with the corners of his eyes for Meca. Meca was missing though, absent from every part of the room. Danal swallowed hard and sat down.

There seemed to be twelve, all white garbed figures sitting on a white platform, about half way up towards the very height of the tower. There were three lights that flashed from the top, sending their lights down into the midst of the crowd, regularly, constantly, flashing. He saw Kirin sitting in the middle of the white-clothed figures. She was the only one who was looking at him.

After what seemed like an eternity, the High Minister Kirin rose to her feet and stretched her long arms out to the crowd. "Join in awareness!" The crowd stood and replied with surprising feeling, "Join in awareness!"

There were a few more words of casual greeting and then Kirin and the other eleven descended from their platform in the sky. They stood in the center and joined hands, forming a circle. They seemed to utter unheard prayers and then they broke hands and walked slowly towards the crowd, all twelve holding out long, spiny fingers.

Kirin said simply, "The tribunal meets."

The crowd seemed hushed and expectant. And then, the most astonishing sight, a large glowing object seemed to form from the lights at the top of the tower, to form into a smooth glowing circle, and then glide slowly downward to come to rest directly in front of Kirin. Danal couldn't believe what he was seeing. The object was round and shiny and appeared to have a black center. It seemed alive.

Kirin began to speak some very foreign sounding words and slowly, oh so slowly, she moved her fingertips back and forth over the strange, glassy object.

I tried to keep my wits about me, as old horror tales played in my mind. My eyes searched the room for some sign of Meca. But he was not here, not here to witness this spectacle of mystery.

Kirin spoke slowly to the crowd, in several different languages. Then she came slowly to stand before me and smile softly, "Danal, it is your time," she said simply and paused. "It is time for you to join, time for your revelation. Do you consent?"

"I will not consent to anything until I know where my partner, Meca, is, and what you want of me." I spoke with panicky desperation.

"Meca is safe, and I, we, want nothing from you."

"I don't believe you!" I said with a sick feeling growing in my stomach.

"Very well," and Kirin motioned to one of a string of very tall men, standing at attention by the entrance. "Bring him," she whispered.

I was too afraid to even think clearly, by then. Old tales and uneasiness were moving through my tired bones, filling my body with a trembling disquiet. Then, only a moment seemed to pass. I looked with fear, as Meca came in, escorted by the white guard, and then my fear turned to terror as I looked at Meca's face. I knew instantly that something had happened. I could see it in the numbness of Meca's eyes.

Meca was led to a chair on the right side of the room. And I was shocked as his eyes never once looked for me, never once met my gaze. He looked only downward. I was afraid.

"Are you satisfied? Meca is alive and will soon feel harmony, when his Opening is complete." Kirin looked at me intently, measuring me silently.

I couldn't think to speak.

"Will you be Opened, Danal, to join with your awareness?"

"No, I said, meekly, "not until I know what will happen ..." My voice trailed off as I ran out of words.

Kirin smiled and turned to my friend, my partner. "Meca?" She looked inquisitive. Meca stepped forward and said, "Yes, I wish to complete my Opening."

I was stunned. I just couldn't believe what I was hearing, but yes, it was Meca's voice, it was Meca speaking. Then everything else seemed to happen very fast, but in slow motion.

"I, Kirin, as High Minister of zone 94, ask for the High Order to live," and she placed the tips of her fingers on the glowing object facing us. It seemed to glow brighter and brighter, a white light coming forth from its black center, a warm light that grew stronger and stronger, flowing out into the room, covering Meca with a brilliant light.

As Kirin said, solemnly, "We give thanks," the light seemed to become a thick, white fog that flowed out through the tower room, dissolving all over us, and filling the air with a strange, sparkling energy. The object itself grew bigger, became intense, and was covered with danc-ing, colored energies. It was so intense, it made my eyes hurt to look at it. It began to appear to look like a shiny screen, filled with multi-colored lights. Surprisingly, even in my great fear, there was something so beautiful about it.

"Meca is ready," Kirin said, gently, as she took Meca's hand, and guided him to stand closer to the screen. The two of them seemed to light up with a gold light as if lightning had struck both of them or, should I say, it seemed to pass from the object into them. I was mesmer-ized.

"Look into the Seeing Glass, Meca, it is your time," Kirin said, as she let go of his hand, and stepped back. Meca moved even closer to the screen. What happened next is hard to describe. I don't know the words to express the force of the experience.

Everything seemed to happen in a whirl. Abruptly, the room became total darkness, and a picture began to appear on the massive globe-like screen. The picture was of a small group of men, eight, I think, sitting in a large piece of land, surrounded by trees. It was a strange sight. The trees looked very strange, they were green. Can you imagine? Green trees! I had never seen green trees before. And the picture looked so intensely real.

There was complete silence in the room as everyone watched the screen, riveted by the men there who seemed to be speaking some strange, foreign tongue. They were dressed very oddly, too. I had never seen anything like it. And they held something in their hands, some sort of container, a small cylinder that they seemed to drink from. Then the men stopped talking and the picture appeared to freeze in time. A flash of light from the screen passed into Kirin and she began to speak.

"You have committed an offense against the High Order, Meca, do you recognize?"

"It ... it is me. The man clothed in blue, is me ... it was my life ... once," Meca said slowly, and there seemed to be tears streaming down his cheeks.

"Yes, Meca, you were called by a different name, then, but it is you. It is the you that lived and breathed on the planet called Earth, in the Earth year of 1979. You left that planet, within the year after this scene, you witness, transpired ... but not before you committed a great offense."

As Kirin stopped speaking, the picture began to move again. All of the young men, including the man in blue, were still sitting in the wooded area, talking loudly, boisterously. Then the man in blue got to his feet clumsily and after taking a long drink from his cylinder, he squeezed it hard and with great laughter, he turned around and hurled it into the trees. All of the other men rose to their feet and followed suit, silvery containers cast gloatingly through the air, falling to the ground in some crude, playful sport. There was a painful, metallic ringing sound as the small missiles hit their target in this strange, unruly game.

The picture was so real and then the scene seemed to freeze once more, this time focusing on the tall man in blue, caught somewhere in time, with a very large grin on his face.

Another flash of light seemed to pass from the screen to Kirin, and one to Meca, lighting them both up. They seemed like three glowing objects in the center of the room. I saw that Meca was crying, he seemed to struggle to stop in order to hear Kirin.

"You have broken one of the most serious laws, Meca. You have sinned against the High Order."

Meca began to weep, wildly, uncontrollably.

Kirin continued on, "You have committed a terrible offense. You have sinned against your mother, a mother that allowed you to live and breathe and gave you life for twenty earth years. You, in return, gave her pain and damage. You hurt her greatly with the deeds you witness here again. Look into that life where your most serious transgression was lived. When you are ready for the removal of that offense, look into the center of the screen where the image was formed."

And then my eyes were filled with the tension of watching the impossible, as I saw Meca, clearly, walk even closer to the middle of the screen and in one short moment, Meca and the man in blue seemed to merge, as an intense light flashed everywhere. Meca seemed, almost, to have walked into the scene and become the man in blue, with a smile on his face.

The picture seemed to fade into a bright glow, glowing with a blue light, and leave the Meca I knew, standing in the center, screaming in pain, and wearing the other man's blue uniform.

It seemed so easy for them both to become one; I was shocked. Meca did not have the other man's smile, though, his face seemed rigid with pain.

Kirin and the other eleven High Ministers stepped forward and each placed a long, elegant finger on the iridescent, blue orb. Each of them seemed to be filled with a blue light, and Kirin began to speak with great force. "The atonement has begun and will continue until the balance of the spirit, who is called Meca, is complete. During the transmutation, he will be allowed the privilege of the Six Lights; he is given the great gift of being allowed to rest during the six moons. During that time, he is free, completely free of the hand of fate. No God of the High Order will see him, it will be as if the spirit of Meca does not exist. The fingers of Karma may not reach in and pluck him from his resting place, the eyes of the Seeing Glass will not be upon him. Only when he steps from the silence of his resting hole, in the light of the seventh moon, will the Law of the High Order be absolute."

The dense white fog seemed to swirl and shake and become a great storm of lights. Colors flashed everywhere as if the Gods of lightning were getting ready to make their grand entrance.

I wanted to say something, I'm not sure what, but I couldn't speak. My heart felt very heavy for my good friend Meca.

Kirin seemed to be speaking directly to the eye-like globe. "We ask for the spirit who is Meca to be Joined in Awareness, and we give thanks."

Then there was a great gust of wind through the tower and a horrible, prolonged, shuddering noise.

The energy appeared to change into shapes and sounds, alive with an exuberant noise. All of a sudden, Meca seemed to be hit by something and fell to the floor, screaming. He cried out!

Trees began to form around him, out of the energy in the air, strange, vivid green trees. They swayed in the strong breeze dancing around Meca, my Meca, who was lying in the middle, writhing in pain. Then something again fell from the top of the tower, hitting him with a tremendous force, and then another object and another. And then a steady stream of small, cylinder-like objects seemed to come hurtling out at him from all directions, over and over and over. Meca's body screamed and shook in agony.

I tried, then, to move and run towards him, to pull him out of the way, but I found that I couldn't move. I literally couldn't get out of my chair. Some unseen force seemed to hold me in place.

The room was alive with this terrible wind and lights, and Meca's soul was voicing its torment. I couldn't stand it. I tried to scream, too, and found no words coming out. But Kirin looked at me and I think, I don't know why, I think she could hear my soundless screaming. I cried out to her to help him. And then I heard Kirin's voice, but coming from inside my head, amidst the great turmoil of the room. "Danal do not struggle so ... this is not your battle."

"But I can't just stand by and watch my friend struggle and suffer. Suffer for what? Does he think that he once lived in this strange man's body? And even if he did, why ... why should he suffer for it now?" I screamed words, in my head, to Kirin and she heard me.

"Meca knows, feels what he suffers for. He knows, also, that this is the hour of his nemesis, his time of reckoning. He seeks balance, Danal, as all men do, in their hearts."

I watched as Meca lay bleeding, silvery bullets with sharp edges hurtling down at him with momentous force, crushing into his body.

I closed my eyes, I couldn't bear to see. I cried, "Help him, Kirin. He was only a young man then. His sin could not have been that horrible to deserve this. Meca is a loving soul, filled with respect."

"He is a loving soul, Danal, and filled with respect ... but once he had no love, no respect for the mother who gave him life. He came in to that life knowing the laws, Danal, as we all do. He was young then, but he knew truth. In some small place within him, it was there but he didn't wish to see it; he made his choice then. There were many gatherings with his friends. He thought he was free then, free to hurt and not care. And they would drink together, then, a liquid that would make them feel the freedom they already had. And he and his friends would smash their empty containers of defiance and leave them to collide with an innocent world, a world that became slowly littered with the symbols of selfishness, disinterest and greed. Yes, they were right, they were free to choose their way. And they knew, too, in that small place deep within them, how many reciprocal actions their choices would create. They did not remember, though, remember the hour when fate has its choice." There was a deep sadness in Kirin's face, then. "They had no remembrance of what fate's turn would bring them. They did not remember, there is no rest before the seventh moon, a moon that was not yet seen on that beautiful planet. They did not want to remember. They wanted to live well and be free to do whatever they wished, to their loving mother, their home planet, a home that was once so green and rich with life. The beings of that time cared not for the needs of their mother and she felt their actions. The planet Earth was allowed to bleed and suffer for a long, long time. And there were few, then, who stood up for her, few who tried to protect her. Many come here to Theorin, though. So many come here, this place will exist always. This is a place that exists at all times, can be reached from many places, many directions. We are an oracle that exists through all time, all worlds, here to assist those whose time has come, who wish to Join in Awareness."

"Watch Meca and you will see, Danal, you will see how your mother, the planet Earth, felt for a very long time."

And I watched until I could watch no longer. I closed my eyes and tried not to hear the sounds. I felt hate for this place, hate for Kirin and the others who allowed this to go on. And then I opened my eyes for a moment and looked at Kirin, looked deep into her eyes. She returned my look and I heard her strong voice, again, flowing into my consciousness.

"I do not do this to him, Danal. I am only one, one who helps, from this place, to assist those beings who look for Theorin. This time will come to an end too, and when it does, Meca will be one again, whole, filled with a balance, a harmony that he chose once to lose. This is a joyous time, Danal, for this is the hour that Meca has chosen, again, chosen harmony and truth now, and the High Order has received him. Would you deny him this time?"

I saw something, then, in Kirin's eyes, that I had never seen before. It was truth and within that truth was a deep caring, a very deep love. I forced myself to look at the Meca I had known for so long, so many journeys together, and I saw that same light, that golden light of truth being born.

I knew, then, that I was ready, ready for a harmony I had never known before, but one I had always missed. I knew my time, too, had finally arrived.

35

THE WORLD OF THEORIN

After three weeks of writing *In The Light Of Another Moon*, I felt as though I had spent the whole time on Theorin. During that time I was as puzzled as Danal and Dr. Meca.

The world of Theorin looked very alien from the resting holes of Kirin, Danal and Meca. Those resting holes were my first vantage points from which to see this strange planet and begin the experience of this compelling story.

Very soon I felt myself filled with that orange light of uneasiness but not illuminated by it. Each new scene, each new event, only made me search harder for understanding.

As I walked the streets with Danal and Meca, I could feel a thick tension in the air. I searched the vacant faces of the passersby but their attention seemed always to be fixed inwards.

My mind kept reaching outward, trying to grasp the significance of my own feelings and the changing scenery. I became super alert, my senses standing on edge. I felt that any second I would feel, hear, smell something that would finally cause it all to make sense.

Not until the ceremony of Opening and Atonement, did I even begin to understand. As Meca viewed moments from his past life on Earth, I remembered the teenagers partying in the woods outside my apartment. The scenes of Meca and his friends in drunken revelry could not have differed much from the scenes outside my window.

I remembered wishing that, one day, those inconsiderate people might feel the consequences of their actions. I wondered if they ever really would. I guess I never dreamed that one day they might seek out that knowledge, might ask to feel the consequences.

Rick devoured this story, reading it twice that first day. He was amazed at the parallels between the kids in the woods outside our apartment and Meca's experiences in a past life on the planet Earth. Rick commented, "You know, it's fascinating the way the writers seem to weave the ordinary events and questions of our lives into the fabric of these other-worldly stories. On the other hand, maybe this is not just a story, maybe it will really happen. Maybe one of the kids in our woods becomes Dr. Meca in a future life and this scenario unfolds in a very distant future time."

Sometimes the stories sent us into long, playful discourses that lasted hours and days.

"When the story was coming through," I recalled, "and the ceremony of atonement was proceeding, I remember feeling much like Danal, pleading in my heart to spare Meca. I could feel Meca's goodness and decency. Even if he had ever been that callous or indifferent in some other life, in this life he was a good and gentle man. Yet I could also feel that it was Meca's very decency that moved him towards this atonement, that made him want to burn away any mistake that might get in the way of the experience of oneness that he was seeking."

"I feel like I've done that," Rick mused as he looked back and inward. "I feel like there were many times in my life when I had to feel the texture and pain of my own wrong doings. It's a very internal process, remembering and feeling, being completely truthful. I don't know that it's a fully conscious process. It's like, I'm working, talking and simply living my normal life while another part of me has crashed on some alien planet where I am given the opportunity to become smooth and clean and free. In this process, something is completed and forgiven. I think that real compassion and deep understanding come from this journey."

"Remember how Kirin said, near the end of the story, that we come into the world balanced and in harmony, and that we are free to disturb that balance and give up that harmony." I added in. "I think that's true. It really seems that we are created in a state of oneness and that we chose to fall from that oneness. In that state of imbalance, restless and uneasy, we find no real rest until we choose our atonement. Maybe we make that choice in the light of another moon."

Rick and I, to this day, still talk about this story. It seems to be one of those priceless and perhaps timeless reminders to us that we always have choice. And it does seem very important to remember that we are free, always free to make choices.

36

A Dream Of Spring

The third week of April arrived, filled with promise and hope. The winter had been long, cold and snowy. Even the days in March seemed to be blown by the wind, one into the other, like dried leaves down long gray streets. But April brought bright, shiny days and just a few warm, still golden days. The returning birds sang of newness, tiny young shoots of grass broke through the dark, rich earth, and distant stands of trees shone in hues of pink and pale green. Spring seemed like a secret dream gradually making itself real.

One quiet night while lying in bed, I thought I could almost feel the Earth as she began to stir and breathe. In the silence, the colors of life were returning in soft silent brush strokes that I could hear as I listened carefully. The dream of spring was filling with the juices and movement, smells and wings of being. The velvet murmur of peepers and crickets lulled me to sleep and into a beautiful dream about a woman, Karen, her world and her dreams.

I had only one dream of Karen, a dream filled with symbols and images that made me take a deep look at reality and dreams. When I sat down to type this story, it came through me like a dream. In one sitting, it wove its way on to paper and into reality. As Karen's story unfolded, I watched her pass from dreams to waking life and back again.

This story is really a room from which to see the interplay of creation and awakening. The story of Karen is truly *The Seeing Room.*

37

FROM THE TIME TUNNEL:
THE SEEING ROOM

She walked slowly through the serene, lush garden, noticing every moment as it passed around her. The perfume of the flowers reached out to blend with her own sweet scent, filling the air with a fresh, green lightness blended with jasmine and rose and spice. It gave her a feeling of expectancy.

Karina's bare arms felt a tingle in the air, as she held the white lace shawl softly to her, draping it over her tawny shoulders. She felt alive, filled with an excitement she had never known before. This would be their night. At last, after all the long years of waiting, longing, yearning, they would finally be together. As she walked along the perfectly manicured path of the garden, she caught a glimpse of the clearing up ahead. And then, there it was, a beautiful, glittering gazebo, silhouetted in the moonlight, the white, lacy wood shining with a silvery glow. Her own castle of white lace, illumined under the kiss of the moon.

She took a long, deep breath and then an even more exciting sight, she saw him all at once. He was up ahead, standing tall, handsome in black, waiting for her alone, waiting in the castle of her dreams. At last, her time had come. Karina had waited so long for this moment, perhaps all her life.

The tall man dressed in black also took a deep breath. He had not seen Karina for over five years now, and they had been five very long years, but in every moment of those difficult years, she had been there with him, her presence sheltered in his heart, her pretty scent filling his dreams each and every night, her perfect face always filling his soul with love for her. Oh how he had longed for her, had reached out for her during so many sleepless nights, nights filled with moonlight but not with Karina. She had been absent from his life for far too long.

As he looked at her great beauty, he wondered how he had endured being away from her for even a moment. He took all of her charm in, drinking deep from her dazzling presence. He watched the white lace caressing her shoulders and he longed to be that wisp of pretty gauze. The lace was like a web of silvery moonlight catching her in its grasp. The white net seemed to become the light radiating from that celestial body, so far away, and the lace and the moon and Karina were all one. Yes, truly, Karina was the moonlight of his life.

As she slowly awakened, the sleep in her eyes made them feel tired and dry, but her eyelashes fluttered with happiness and fulfillment, at least until she opened her eyes completely and then it all came back to her.

Dreaming, again, but what a dream it had been! As Karen turned off the alarm and turned on the coffee, there was still so much moonlight in her eyes. Aah, it was another day though, she sighed, and they weren't much fun. It was the nights she looked forward to, Karen knew, but they were far, far too short.

This would be a worse day than usual, she remembered, the last day of school, and her students would be out for the summer and Karen, where would she be? She just wasn't sure.

"Karen!" Terry greeted her in the hall, "Where are you bound for this summer? Gonna miss the old school halls?"

"I … I think I'll be staying here in town, Terry, Just having a quiet summer."

"Not me, I'm bound for the sea, two months of sailing, free as a bird, enjoying the salt air in my face and ports of call filled with wine, women and song. I can't believe you're just staying here in town. You ought to get out, do something … fall will be here soon enough, and you'll be back facing these same, stuffy walls."

"I really like having the quietness, Terry ... but you have a wonderful, wonderful time and I'll see you in a few months."

"Okay, kid." Terry looked at her as if she was part of these old school walls.

"And I guess," Karen thought, "I am."

It was not as if she hadn't any place to go. An old friend had asked her to come to her summer place for a visit. But Karen hadn't even bothered to write and decline. Actually, she had forgot. It would be too much trouble, too noisy there, anyway. Her friend, Jane, had two very young children now and Karen could imagine what kind of summer it would be with them. I would so much rather stay right here in town, she thought, where it's quiet, no change, just lazy days and even better nights. Yes, this is a place where I can relax, she thought, and dream peacefully.

Summer passed so slowly in her dreams. Karen walked to the park early in July and wondered why she felt a little out of sorts, restless.

"I should be happy," she thought, "I have everything. I'm a very good teacher. I make very good money. And I live in a very nice, quiet neighborhood."

Her life always felt a little pale but she didn't usually mind. She knew what her life was and she was used to it, had grown into it, counted on it, had begun to think that her life was all there was and that everything is just the way it should be.

But not today. On this very clear July morning, it was as if contentment had left all at once, had flown away, leaving a strange space, a hole filled with only air, the air of Karen's life.

She didn't understand it but she immediately had the feeling not to look in the hole; she knew instinctively, it was too deep to see the bottom. So Karen shrugged her tawny shoulders and dismissed the feeling, her life and the world.

She felt far away as she walked through the park and even further away as she began to saunter home, back to the small brown house that was her castle. Karen's feet did not touch the ground, nor her eyes, nor her mind, nor her spirit, they were all lost, out dancing in a dream. So it was awhile before she realized she was surrounded by flashing red lights.

So slowly, the moving brightness seemed to invade her dream world, until she could no longer fight off the enemy of light. When she awakened, she snapped to attention like an officer in the war coming to life.

Her house was on fire, her house was on fire! The words seemed to playfully fly past her, only to land squarely in the center of her mind with a great noise. "My God, my house is on fire," she screamed, as she noticed at last the tall men in black, climbing on glowing ladders into the windows of her castle.

Every door barricaded with red light, a dark gray smoke rushing out of the chimney, a war going on in her house, in her castle, in her world. And Karen watched with eyes wide open, lids filled with the moistness of all that light, her heart on fire, caught at last between two worlds, as one of them slowly, so slowly, burned to the ground. She watched every moment of the labor. She caught every drop of water, streaming from the hose, in her own desperate gaze. She felt as if she too was smoldering as the wood crackled, along with the dryness of her own tired bones. The scorching blaze spread deep inside her, lighting up the hole within. And then, finally, at long last, she could see bottom. Her time had come. Karen's fortress had burnt to the ground. The hot embers burning for what seemed like forever. And it was such a long time before the coolness came.

When she moved to her friend Jane's summer place, a few days later, Karen took with her only the beautiful scars from those burning coals of her world. Nothing else had survived the fire. There was no baggage, no clothes, not even a bit of her white lace curtains left.

Karen felt a new freedom in her bones, a yearning to see new ports of call. And she wondered why the world looked so green. As she watched, her eyes filled with a new openness on the trip to Jane's house.

Karen was happy to meet the children at last. She began to look forward to a summer filled with their sparkling eyes, long walks on the beach and the feeling of salt air on her face.

There was one thing that really excited her more than anything else, though, sent a feeling of joy all through her, gave her the idea that perhaps now her life had really just begun. It was the garden in Jane's back yard, so many paths of lush greenness and a white gazebo just waiting in the center.

Karen knew that this was a place where her scars could all heal. At last, her time had come.

38

THE UNDENIABLE NOW

April opened into May like eyes opening in the first rays of morning light. Bursts of bright yellow forsythias bloomed overnight and hesitant, new lilacs blossomed fragrantly as the dream of spring became real and felt. What, only weeks ago, had been wishes and hopes, began to fill with color and warmth. And as the dream took its first breath, made its first sounds, I found it even more wonderful than I had remembered.

As I felt spring take shape, it reminded me of the feelings that I experience as I enter trance. At first there are only sweet memories of the feelings and the journey, then hints and whispers that tantalize the senses, and then finally I am floating thankfully and drifting freely into the quiet thickness of the undeniable now.

The morning after typing "The Seeing Room", I sat at the kitchen table in the transparent warmth of the sun filtering through the window, reading the story over and over. I rubbed my thumb across the thin edge of one of the crisp, white typewritten pages and listened to the soft papery sound. The sunlight made the paper nearly luminous and the bright light made my eyes just a little sleepy as I drifted into the warmth and the light and the sound. I felt my body ease back in the chair, my shoulders dropped a little. I must have put the pages down because I remember feeling the warmth of one hand on the other resting in my lap.

I found myself in a kind of seeing room in my inner world. My body was so comfortable that the experience of being in a body drifted away. In this seeing room I watched the characters, Karen and her friends, living in the scenes of their story. I not only saw them, but I could feel their feelings and know their dreams.

As I watched Karen, I wondered about her life, her dreams. I felt the tremendous power of her dreaming, the energy of her imagination. Karen played boldly in her dreams, never limited her choices and actions. And yet in her waking life there seemed to be such hesitance. I could feel the power of her imagination banging on the door of her waking life.

In her daily life Karen seemed stuck, trapped in her beliefs and apprehension. There seemed to be such a conflict between her two worlds. And I could feel that conflict churning and smoldering under the surface.

I had this unconscious sense that Karen's world was ready to give birth to her dreams, her dreams had come full term. And there was a point in this process when I felt that Karen's world could have changed more easily, when her dreams could have simply flowed into existence. An easy birth, a painful birth, they teetered back and forth. Her waking world felt stiff and inflexible, and when it burned down, it seemed like it needed to burn. I could feel the intense relief.

Suddenly I felt the chair beneath me and the floor under my feet. It was as if I had flowed back into the chair, into the kitchen, back into the light. When I got up and walked out on to the deck, I felt that I knew more about the interplay between dreams and the waking world. I felt that I had grasped some great truth on the tip of my mind. But I was forgetting just how it felt, forgetting it like dreams that slip quietly back into the night. I wanted to retrace my steps, reassemble the puzzle, remember the formula, but I had left the seeing room and I had returned to my own castle and my own dreams.

39

THE TREE HOUSE

I remember this particular morning, not so much for its sparkle or brilliance, but for the comfort of its sameness. It was one of those days that show me, again, that the doors to perception and change are often waiting in the simplicity of the ordinary.

I was sitting on the porch of the "tree house" (that's what Rick and I called our third floor apartment that seemed suspended high in the trees) just daydreaming, as the morning slowly unfolded. The warm, velvet soft breeze played lightly on my face and gently moved my hair.

It was Sunday morning and life in the apartment complex stirred gradually, purposely slow, lazy, happy not to be rushing off to work or school. The breeze carried in its warm folds smells of breakfast cooking, whiffs of freshly cut grass, the scents of new flowers, and sounds, sounds of children eager to play, church bells calling in the flocks, fluttering leaves that sounded like ocean waves when I shut my eyes, and the sound of Rick playing his guitar in the bedroom. I remember thinking that Rick must be writing a song, responding to some inspiration, or he wouldn't be playing so early.

As I opened up my senses, smells, sounds, sights, feelings, time seemed to stand still. The moment expanded like a balloon endlessly inflating, filling with this breath of experience and information. I felt as if the boundaries of *me*, were pushing out to include more and more, past the porch, out into the trees, and then in the blink of an eye, into spaces and scenes that, a moment ago, weren't there, at least not in my physical world. This was very different from simply entering my imagination or traveling to another reality. I was still perceiving my world, the porch, the apartment, the trees, but in addition I was seeing another world that seemed to occupy the same space, superimposed over my ordinary reality.

I slowly recognized this other world as a world that I had visited in a dream, just hours before I had awakened. Almost instinctively, I rose and stepped into the apartment to get my notebook and pen. I could see my body passing through objects that appeared to be solid in this other world, while I honored the solidness of other objects, objects like my dining room table and kitchen counter. I picked my way through the landscapes of both realities, retrieved my writing implements, and returned carefully to the porch. Sitting down with writing materials in hand seemed to be the signal that opened the door and helped me to completely enter that alternate reality. It was as though I had chosen, in that moment, to enter into that other world, fully, and to witness and record the story that was being given to me.

I wrote with single-mindedness, hardly stopping to catch my breath. Even when I did look up for a moment's rest, my eyes came to rest on the fixtures of this other place, this nameless woman's apartment, her packed bags and the worn old clock.

I felt her words touch me and make me wonder at her fears, her guilt. I tried to look into her heart, to feel her feelings, but although I could share her emotions, I couldn't sense their source.

I wrote on. The story flowed like a stream of music from one time to another, or one world to another. And I was traveling and listening in that other world. I listened to the last words of the story, watched them as I wrote them on this paper in my world. But so much of me was still there, there with those last feelings, with those last lines of this golden tale. Somewhere in the back of my mind, I could hear Rick's footsteps as he walked towards me from the bedroom. He had been lost in some musical world of notes and chords, verses and refrains. Yet when he spoke to me softly, through the screen door, I nearly jumped out of my chair. It was as if I was still so much in this other world, this other time, that I somehow thought that Rick wouldn't be able to see me.

For a moment, I felt somehow naked, so visible, so physical. And Rick understood, in his way, without his asking or my explaining. We both had felt a little lost in time, here, and yet off somewhere else. Yet I could sense that we never really become lost in time. Time remains the same. Time gives us the gift of change and as you will read next, *Time Has A Golden Face.*

40

FROM *THE TIME TUNNEL:*

TIME HAS A GOLDEN FACE

As I packed all of my possessions in the worn, brown leather bag, I felt a terrible uneasiness. I wanted to stop and unpack everything, without actually having to see myself do this, as if I'd never started to pack in the first place.

I could change my mind. I might not leave at all. I kept my hands over the large bag without touching its soft, plying leather, holding them there for several minutes without moving. Then I noticed the long passage of time.

Out of the corner of my eye, I saw the small, golden clock my grandmother had given me, so long ago. The beautiful little timepiece was partly hidden under the clutter of the past twenty years of my life, tucked back, a little too far away to see, but just peeking out enough so that its golden face caught my attention.

I hadn't seen the tiny clock for a long time. I had forgotten I even owned it. And there it was, hiding on the shelf behind the baby pictures, my long strands of pearl beads and a beautiful multi-colored paper bird that someone had given me a long time ago. I forgot who. The bird's wings were hidden behind clear blue bottles filled with creamy, mysterious liquids that I carefully put on my face each and every day, to cover, to beautify and to protect. Tall blue bottles, that even I could hide behind.

I reached out and took the intricate little clock out from behind its dusty world. I thought how it is that time has this way of hiding from all of us, and how it also has the ability to bring each of us out of hiding whenever it chooses to. The clock was still keeping time; somehow I knew it would be. The perfect hands said four o'clock and I realized that if I didn't leave soon, I would miss the plane.

A thin wave of guilt stabbed at my heart. How could I have even thought of not going? My grandmother needed me now. She had begged me to come to her for the last three years and I, I had refused, had read all of her letters, so quickly, afraid to hear the warnings between the words, not ever being able to acknowledge her pain; I couldn't read them, hear them. I didn't want to. But now, I told myself, I would have the courage to hear. No matter what that meant to me, or to her, I would look. For the first time in my life, I would not only notice and hear, I would allow myself to go back.

My bag full of haphazard possessions was difficult to close up, crammed so tightly with the baggage of my world. I lifted the satchel slowly, surprised at the weight, and more surprised at the strange heaviness that seemed to be moving all through me. I was afraid but I knew more surely than anything I'd ever known before, that this was a journey I must make.

I walked towards the door carrying the solid bag filled with the lead from my life, and in my left hand I held the tiny gold clock securely in the palm of my hand. As I felt its smooth, shiny face, it gave me the courage to take the first step and walk through the door. I was on my way back to a world I hadn't acknowledged for a long, long time.

The trip itself was filled with a thousand thoughts, thoughts I allowed myself, and all the thoughts I didn't want to have.

I had always wanted to visit Norvalai, who didn't, but not like this. Actually, I have always been more than intensely interested in Norvalai. I have always longed to go there, to see the great city itself, perhaps the greatest city of our time, and of course to see the only wonder of the world that is left there, the spectacle they call Tora.

Now I would have a chance but my excitement was dimmed by the thought of seeing my grandmother. I still didn't want to face her. I hadn't wanted to see her for a long time and now, even though she had moved to Norvalai, I wasn't sure if I was ready yet.

There had been so much pain between us, for all these years, pain I knew I carried with me. But I thought I had put the feelings in a box and locked it, and put it so far away, that I would never, ever, have to look at their faces again. I had learned a long time ago that certain feelings had horrible faces, features too hideous to gaze upon. Better to cover them up, protect them, hide them away forever.

It was hard to even think about those times when we had been so close, when there was nothing bad between us, only good times to remember, then. I had never known who my real mother was. The only kindness I ever knew as a child was from the wise old woman who raised me, the woman I called Grandmother, who took care of me, who tried to give me everything, all the love, strength, peace and beauty that were part of her.

And now that gentle soul would be leaving soon and she wanted to see me. And now that she was dying, could I bear to see her? And the worst question, the one I tried always to hide at the very bottom of the box, it seemed to echo now through every bone; would she ever, ever forgive me?

When I arrived in Norvalai, I felt like I had been catapulted into a different time. The great city was so different from the small villages where I had always lived. I was struck by its size and the people! I felt as if I'd never seen so many people in one place.

I felt mesmerized by the sounds and all the activity around me. I think it hit me all at once. Here I am, finally, actually here in Norvalai, the only large city left on our planet. I think a part of me thought that I would never really get here. Why, I had only known one other person who had visited here.

I felt high with excitement. I walked slowly through the city, feeling more and more elated, staring at the massive, metal buildings gleaming under the powerful light of the sun.

I enjoyed walking aimlessly for a long time. Then slowly I began to feel a little dazed. I began to feel as if the light was too bright in my eyes, the sounds too loud in my ears, and the smoky air all around me began to make me feel quite heavy.

The afternoon had arrived and I knew I should begin finding directions to the old part of the city where my grandmother now lived. But I began to feel so tired and hot. I found myself wandering into a shiny building where I saw an indoor park, filled with benches and even more people relaxing in the refreshing indoor air. So I sat down to rest for a while next to an old, old lady who was happily eating rice and drinking tea. As I found myself staring at the hands holding the cup of rice, I realized how hungry I had become.

She had such a nice, kind smile as she looked up at me, feeling my eyes on her rice. "You will have some?" she said slowly, looking deeply into my eyes.

"No, I couldn't," I replied, wistfully.

"Please you look hungry," and she placed the cup in my left hand, motioning me to eat with her quick fingers.

As I began to eat, she began to talk, still smiling.

"You are not from here, you have come for a visit … or will you stay?"

"Only a visit," I talked between mouthfuls.

"Then you come to see Tora. You are one of the lucky ones who have come, now, while Tora is still alive."

"Well yes, I would like very much to see it while I am here sometime, but I am only here for a short visit … and I am really here to see my grandmother," I said halfheartedly, remembering, feeling a little faint still from the heat lingering outside.

The old lady smiled once more, and I don't know why, but I had the feeling that she knew all about me, that she knew my fears and sadness. I think somehow, my anxiety revealed itself to her, in my face.

"But you don't want to see her, do you?" And she looked so deep into my eyes that I wanted to run back out again into the blinding sun, just to get away from the light in her sharp face. But I didn't move.

Instead, I told her my story. I told her all about my grandmother and about me, and she listened so intently, with her beautiful face always smiling, always gentle. And somehow, I didn't have to tell her everything. She already knew.

I finished all of her rice and I drank all of her cool tea and I poured out the contents of the box to her, the one I always carried with me in my heart. And she listened.

When my aching words ran out, she put her hands on mine and said simply, "I know, we are all the same. It will be all right now. The time has come for you to heal. You must always remember that time will forgive."

I asked for directions to the old part of the city and she seemed to know it well. I was just about to start off when she grabbed my arm and stopped me.

"You will go to Tora first, to see it now, while you are here."

"I may go sometime before I leave but I should get on with my journey now." I was beginning to nervously feel the lateness of the day.

"No," she said, for the first time not smiling, "Tora is the next stop on your journey. You must go there first ... and then you will be free, free to take all the next steps of the rest of your life. I will walk part way with you and show you," she said.

She was so determined, I didn't have the heart to argue. I found myself back on the scorching street, walking with her into the glare of the sun just beginning to set.

It wasn't very long before we arrived. We were really closer than I had known. I said good-bye to the lady and just as she left me, she handed me a small, worn piece of folded-up, crinkly paper.

"From an old book," she said. "It is my favorite and I know all the words by heart. But don't read until after you have seen Tora and then you will understand. Tora is magnificent!" And she smiled the most golden smile I had ever seen. Then she pointed me down to the end of a long and busy road and she disappeared. One minute she was here and the next minute the old lady was gone.

Even as I approached, the sight of the glass building was beautiful, sparkling within sight of the sun now falling gently in the sky. I felt a tremendous excitement as I stood in the crowd lined up waiting to go in and see Tora, perhaps the most marvelous wonder on the planet. I didn't know what it would be like. I couldn't even imagine. I had seen pictures, of course, but they seemed unreal, like something that couldn't really exist. But Tora did exist, there was only one on the planet and I was going to see it, now, for myself.

The tall transparent building was seven floors high and I could see the people on each floor through the clear, shiny walls.

As the line of sightseers entered, we walked slowly into a great glass hallway, circling gracefully upward. The hall seemed to form a ramp that moved slowly in a circle inside of the building, with Tora in the center.

As I kept walking upward, around the bend of the circle, the wall opened up in front of us and the rest of the ramp was completely open, and there began to be a very strange odor. It was like nothing I had ever smelled before. It was a strong, fresh odor and it seemed familiar in some strange way, and it was wonderful! I wanted to keep breathing and breathing all the air filled with this heavy scent of Tora.

As I eased ahead in line, I suddenly caught a glimpse and then it slowly came into full view. I think my heart stopped. No, maybe it was my life that stopped. For one beautiful moment, I caught my breath and I think time really did stand still! It was breathtaking! I was really here! I was really standing in front of Tora, the only real, living tree left on the planet. A living, breathing tree with strong roots that went deep into the ground, old roots that went deep into the heart of the planet.

The large brown and gray trunk was at least two stories high, before even the first branch, and as I looked up, I could see many branches and all the green, glistening leaves reaching up to almost the very top of the glass sky.

I felt like I was seeing a mythical creature from another time, and I guess maybe I was. I wondered why we had ever allowed these creatures from the past to be slain, trees that had lived so fully, once, in a long ago past that must have been glorious. I ached with intense pain as I gazed at this beautiful creature of a tree, still clinging to life. Then I wondered if they would ever, ever forgive us.

It was so hard to believe that once the planet was covered with trees very much like this one. And so many other different kinds too, trees that had white bark and ones that had red leaves. At least that's what the history books told us.

As I walked on each glass platform, on every level surrounding Tora, I wanted so much to believe. And as I reached the very top platform, I looked down and the setting sun shot through the glass walls, lighting up the building, like a crystal glowing with an infinite number of facets, all green and the deepest gold. It was as if a fire was glowing in the very heart of this tall, transparent building and its golden, crystalline energy flew out through the invisible walls, traveling gently in every direction. It seemed to capture the melting rays from the sun and struggled to burn even stronger. It was a green fire.

When I looked into the top of the shiny, yellow-green leaves, something in me remembered. I knew, in every part of myself, that once the world had been filled with these green, glowing creatures, shining with life.

I felt a kinship with Tora and in that moment, I gave that exquisite tree my heart and my solemn pledge that, for the rest of my life, this vision of Tora would always be with me and I would carry it like a treasure and share it with every other soul that I met along the way.

I knew then, that I would always remember this real sign of a life once flowing and alive, on a loving planet. And I so wanted to keep that beautiful, green fire alive.

I stood on the top platform, suspended in the sky. And my life felt like it, too, was suspended, suspended in a great, vast, curious building, the world.

Suddenly I remembered the yellowed paper in my pocket. Unfolding it carefully, I discovered it was a poem. It was called, "A Gift From Time."

A Gift From Time

Time glitters
not for a moment
but for all eternity.
No one moment is ever lost, no one thing ever dies,
but only lives and looks for its own place
in the golden halls of time.

We think things change
they do not
it is us who change.
Time remains the same, forever undisturbed.
Always ready to show us many moods,
only waiting for us to stop and enjoy.

The long road through the halls is filled with questions
and answers.
When we cry, time is there and smiles with patience,
wiping our tears away with minutes and hours and days.
The great continuance hides from us,
forcing us to show our hand, urging us to show ourselves.
How powerfully kind is time.

Always there watching for us,
with slow, easy smiles of compassion,
gentle hands reaching out to us,
giving us quick movements of joy and peace and wisdom.
And there is always the gift of change,
wrapped in the arms of the kindness of time.

Sometimes flashing for a moment,
then standing quietly still for a thousand more,
time always reeks with the past,
and is filled with the gentle scent of the future,
but only ever really lives
right here and now, with us.

Time glitters
not for a moment
but for all eternity.
Shimmering facets flying by us at regular intervals.
So perfect is time and so generous,
time gives with abandon, and always, always forgives.

As I read the last words, I leaned over the glass wall and
allowed my tears to fall on the perfect leaves of that beautiful tree. And I cried for one, very long moment. I cried for
Tora, left alone on a dying planet. And I cried for my
grandmother and for myself and for all who are left alone,
uncared for, left alone to die. I cried for all the trees that
had already gone on and I wondered if they would forgive
us, someday. I hoped, with all my heart, that we would
always hold the vision of the light of this exquisite living
tree in our minds forever. There had to be some place in
the halls of time for this precious green life.

I felt like I left the burden of my life there, at the foot of
Tora, that day. I was finally able to throw out my old box
of pain. I had ached for my grandmother who, like the
beautiful trees that once lived so fully, had been left alone
for so long, to die. I ached with all the bad feelings between us. But I knew, then, that she would forgive me.
And I forgave myself. I was filled with the sense that time
would eventually forgive all of us. I was ready now to
begin nourishing all that was left.

I held my grandmother's tiny clock in both hands and
for the first time, I really felt her love and the love time
must have for each of us. I knew then, time glitters, so full
of the golden face of love.

41

Heaven On Earth

I could feel my own, very real tears, hot and then cold, as they streaked down my face. I finished typing the last few lines of "Time Has A Golden Face" and grabbed for a tissue to dab at my crying eyes. I pushed away from the table, away from the story and away from my feelings. I felt like I was running in the blinding sun, down a crowded hot street, running away from Norvalai with tears flooding my eyes and blurring my vision.

I felt the lingering feelings of the woman as she let her tears fall on the great tree. Her deep sense of sadness and forgiveness and wonder, all hopelessly blended together as emotion that only tears could relieve. Her feelings, as they mixed with mine, felt simply too much to bear. I was tired, tired of experiencing the lives and emotions of these people from other worlds and times.

I got up from the table and walked out on the deck. I sat down on the worn, blue directors chair that remained there from my morning coffee break, that waited there to hold my tired body as if it knew my ache and my exhaustion. The faded fabric seemed to hug me as I sat and stared up through the leafy branches of the tall oak, through the shifting spaces between leaves and worlds, into the deep blue of an endless sky. I felt the journey of the book coming to a close and yet, at the same time, I felt the infinite press of stories and beings and worlds that awaited my visit, yearning to have their tales told, their lives known.

I knew that I would tell their stories, that I had promised to witness their moments of awakening and pass them on and in to my world. But I could also sense the need to rest and recoup my energy. I resolved to set aside some time for healing and lightness and fun. I envisioned reading, movies, long walks with Rick, rides in the car, and simply time to think and put this nearly whole experience into perspective.

Later that afternoon, I picked up a magazine to indulge in some light reading. I thumbed through the pages mindlessly, only to be greeted by an article on the world's rain forests. I wanted to turn away from it, to hurry on to something else, but something in me said "have courage," and so I began reading. The article was very long and somewhat technical and as I suspected, it was frightening.

I read that nearly one half of the planet's species live in the rain forests, and that the rain forests are largely responsible for replenishing the Earth's oxygen. The article said that the rain forests are being cut and burned at the rate of twenty-five to fifty acres every minute and at that rate, one fifth of the planet's species could be lost in the next twenty-five years. I read that there are hundreds of undiscovered plant and animal species that may vanish in this great destruction before we even know of them. Many of the plant species could be the basis of some wonderful medicine, some important, long awaited cure.

When I finished reading, I was filled with panic, anger and profound sadness. How could we be doing this to our home? Why would we do these things to our warm and beautiful planet? The panic, sadness and anger swirled through my thoughts, pulsed through my body, joined by these seemingly unanswerable questions. There was a moment when I could have easily thrown up my hands in despair, could have given into depression or become completely overwhelmed, but I didn't. In that moment, I felt something shift inside me. I took a deep breath and imagined our beautiful blue planet turning silently in a velvet black space and I surrounded her in white light, embraced her with my hope and desire for healing.

As the week passed, I tried to stay in a positive place, tried to imagine solutions and alternatives. It seemed to me immensely important that I keep my heart and mind open. I consciously nurtured hopeful thoughts and day dreams, as if I were trying to dream into being an alternate path ahead. At times I felt as though I had so little power over these enormous planetary issues. I was only one person. And then I would remember that there is always love and imagination and that I always have that to give.

The days passed slowly and it seemed that in every newspaper, in each magazine, on television programs and in conversations with friends, I was drawn to examples of the planet in decline, almost barraged by information on ecological destruction. I felt as though our Mother Earth was calling and writing, fearful of her possible demise, wanting us nearby.

Rick and I found ourselves more often in discussions about the condition of our planet. Rick felt intensely moved by this latest story and said he'd been finding his attention being drawn to information on the state of our ecology. Even sitting in the dentist's office, he would discover another magazine story on some aspect of our planet's health.

On a quiet Sunday evening we settled in to watch some television. We were a little tired and hoping to find some humor on the tube. We tuned in immediately to a documentary on acid rain. We looked at each other in disbelief and without saying a word we both knew that we were thinking the same thoughts. The thoughts would be worded, "Oh no! ... let's change the channel ... OK ... I guess we're supposed to watch this for some reason."

We sat back and watched this disturbing report. There were vivid pictures of forests, all over our country, that are dying, poisoned by the products of our industry and transportation. There were scenes of European forests where the problem is even worse. In Germany, half of all the trees are dying. Even the Black Forest, the setting for many children's stories, is badly damaged. The aerial views of thousands of acres of withering trees were stunning.

"Through the magic of our own technology, we can see the extent of the harm we have done with our own technology," Rick said in amazement. Sometimes it feels like we've already gone over the edge, past the point of no return. And yet, because this damage seems to extend further than we can physically reach … it causes us to reach beyond the physical. Maybe we have to reach a little higher and deeper by sending our healing intentions and asking for help in prayer."

I half remembered a passage that I'll paraphrase here. We are so inextricably a part of this planet, so much a strand in this web of life, that we cannot harm it without harming ourselves. "Maybe as we heal ourselves, we begin to heal the web of life … as we see our true place in the universe, we can respond to it," I said, feeling more hopeful.

As the weeks passed, we were continuously confronted with more images of our planet and her wounds and pain. Waves of emotion welled up in each of us. I remember times when we were more angry than sad and days when we were more confused than angry. I felt as though a storm of information and emotion blew furiously over our lives and we had to ride the storm out, find a way to survive.

As we reflected back on the story of Tora, the young woman and her grandmother, we found direction hidden in its conversations, events and metaphors. There seems to be a great conflict in our hearts, hearts filled with pain and guilt and not nearly enough forgiveness. The state of our Mother Earth is a reflection of our inner world and all its conflict.

The story suggests that time will forgive us, even if we turn our planet into a living hell. It is after all our planet, our school, our stage.

We could also make a heaven of Earth. We could nurture the love in our hearts and let it shine out into the world. We could create so much light that we could all truly see what we are doing. And in the light of a new day we could simply change our direction. We could undo the harm that has been done and find gentler ways of living. We could truly find our place in the golden halls of time.

What is stopping us? What is the conflict that has burdened our hearts and clouded our vision? Are we like the nameless woman in the story, weighed down by some past pain and guilt, colored by some vague sense of unworthiness and lacking faith in forgiveness? It seems that like her, we are deafened by our guilt and sadness and barely able to hear our Mother's dying cry for love and solace.

Those were the questions that battered us during this storm of emotions. Rick and I were trying hard to understand the dilemma of our planet, not really expecting answers, but trying to deepen our understanding.

I remember asking, "Is this guilt or shame about wrongs done in childhood, or does it reach back even further into past existence's? Do we feel, somewhere deep inside, that we've done the unforgivable and that we are not worthy of love and healing?"

"I think that's it," Rick responded, "This old forgotten shame distorts our relationship to forgiveness, so forgiveness sometimes seems nearly impossible for us. We find it very difficult to forgive others and more difficult to accept forgiveness ... and how often can we actually forgive ourselves? It seems sometimes that we are so heavy with shame and the past, that we are often unable to see the perfection of the present moment as it glitters in front of us."

"I think we fail to see that time is vast enough to contain infinite forgiveness, endless solutions and perfect alternatives. There are paths that naturally take us away from greed and fear and toward our love and faith." As I said this, I could feel our spirit guides there with us, listening. I sat back, for a moment and drifted into that place inside me where I can see and hear them. They too were discussing this subject amongst themselves and appreciating us for our willingness to delve into these difficult questions and feelings. I could feel them encouraging us in our explorations and in our search for solutions.

Let me climb out of my story and speak with you, dear reader, for just a moment. After all we are so much alike, each of us on journeys of discovery. I'm sure you see our planet ailing, hear her cries. Do you find yourself sometimes in despair, overwhelmed by the immensity of it all.

Do you sometimes ask, "What can I do? Where do we start?"

My answer would be this. There are some people who are working on various levels, fighting for the survival of the planet. Some are involved in finding alternative technical solutions, like solar power and other alternative power sources, recycling technologies and more efficient heating and lighting. Some are educating us about pollution while others call polluters to task. There are those raising money to protect the wilderness and endangered species. Some are simply learning to consume fewer goods and use safer products like biodegradable cleaners. Many people donate as much time and/or money to people and organizations who are making a difference. These choices can make a difference. But there is an even deeper change that must take place.

We must begin to genuinely heal ourselves, our pains and shames and despairs. We must come to peace with ourselves and feel that we are worthy of this beautiful planet before we can respond wholeheartedly to her needs. The process of realizing this worthiness is a process of forgiving one's self and humanity and God. It is a journey of truly growing up. It seems to me that each of us needs to look deep into our hearts and lives and find the pain and shame. We need to try as many techniques as possible to let go of and heal this pain. We need to free ourselves of these excuses because this pain and shame is ultimately an excuse not to care, not to hope, and not to expect the very best from life.

Once we let go of our shame and excuses, we find in their place room for courage. When we learn to truly love ourselves, not in some narcissistic way but in a very real, conscious way, in a manner that allows for mistakes, feelings and forgiveness, we will truly want answers and dare to confront these problems of our time. After all these problems are only opportunities to grow and love.

I believe that it will take an enormous amount of courage and love to meet these pressing issues. It takes courage and love to even see the pain of our Mother Earth.

We will have to be strong to remain focused and not become despondent. It will take clarity and self love to get off this treadmill of mindless conformity and out of this rat race of stylish over-consumption. It will take strength to see that we are not victims and that our world and its environment is a reflection of our dreams and hopes and consciousness. We have to dare to hope and dream and think differently. It will take courage and compassion to listen to our Mother Earth, to hear her pain and to respond to it, not as angry, guilty children but as strong loving adults. It requires strength to accept the forgiveness that is ours.

In the end, we will have faith enough to open our eyes and look straight into the golden face of time.

42

INTO THE HEART OF TIME

Summer came slowly and unfolded like an earthy colored blanket on the emerald grass, a place to lie down and watch the movement of the clouds and of my life. It's really only in summer that I relax, only in the warmth and slower pace. I sit and muse in summer and I seem to see and hear and think more clearly.

On a morning in late June, I sat on the deck in my baggy director's chair, looking out through the trees now filled in with fresh green leaves. The trees seemed to gather around me, creating a private space, a safe place for me to dream in. My thoughts were drifting back over the past year's events. I could feel intuitively that a cycle of stories had been completed. These stories would some day comprise a book or collection, I hadn't decided which.

I drifted back over the stories, recalling each one, savoring the feeling that each one had left in my heart. Each story had a particular feel, a unique scent, special talents (like a child has gifts, potentials). Each story had changed me in some way, each had opened me up more to life and to its mystery.

I glanced at the newspaper on the floor at my feet and at the date at the top of the page. I looked at the date, thought back to the first story and back to the ending of the last story, and realized that this cycle of stories had taken one year, almost to the day. In some respects the year had passed too quickly and yet, it was as though ten years of growth had been squeezed into that year. I sat back in the morning sun and savored the closing of the circle, a circle that contained my promise to the Eagle, the stories, the writer's group, my journey with Rick, buckets of tears and my soul that had grown considerably. Now What?

Rick was standing at the table pouring coffee into his mug. "What'd you say honey? I didn't hear you," he called through the screen door.

I hadn't realized that I had asked my question out loud. "Oh ... I was just thinking out loud, I guess. I just realized that we've finished one major part of our agreement ... we've completed a cycle of one year and a group of thirteen stories. I don't know if I ever really thought we'd get this far. And now here we are ... now what?"

It was a small, seemingly simple question, and yet it took us the next two months of long discussions and deliberation before we decided on the format for our book.

We knew that the stories were very special. From the very first story, we sensed that something very important was being given to us, and through us to the world. As each story slid delicately though its portal in time, it became evident to us that these stories were like living myths. Each story, though very personal and unique, portrayed the universal theme of transformation. The stories did, like all true myths, describe what it is like to leap from childhood to manhood and womanhood, from loneliness to love, from fear into faith, from darkness into light. The stories described this journey of transformation as a journey of healing the human spirit.

We at first thought we might publish our stories as a collection of myths or short stories. And then it dawned on us that there was another story to be told and that was the story of our personal journey through this time and these events. We decided to tell our own story.

The task of writing this story fell to Rick, and Rick was both excited and hesitant. He wanted to write our story but he wasn't sure he was able, pointing out how different songwriting was from prose. I felt that he could and I urged him on, giving him all my personal notes and journal so that he could remember the chronology of events and all my personal thoughts and feelings about the past year.

I thought then, as I still do, that Rick was the perfect person to tell our very personal story. But Rick's struggle with his doubts about his own writing ability emerged from time to time during his writing of our story. We were fortunate that our spirit guides were willing to step in and help Rick with his struggle.

On a cool September night, just after midnight, we laid in bed talking about Rick's work on the book. He had been working on our story for nearly a month, through mornings and evenings when he seemed confidant, almost driven, and through times when he appeared pensive and hesitant. Rick was voicing some of his personal doubts when, all of a sudden, we both noticed a shift in the energy in the room. The air appeared to be moving and textured and bright sparkles were visible above us near the ceiling. These changes often signal the presence of our spirit guides and we both know that we are free to disregard them or to tune into them and establish a kind of link for communication. Rick suggested that we talk with them.

I drifted into that place inside me where I can communicate with my spirit friends. It sometimes takes me an hour to reach that place and sometimes it is almost instant. On this evening it took only a few moments for me to feel their presence more fully and to hear their words. They began by commenting on a question that Rick had voiced earlier in the evening. He was questioning whether our choice of book formats was a wise one or if we should publish simply a collection of stories.

"There are, of course, many choices open to you, as to style and format. The choice you have made is a good one," they began. "Songmaster Rick (the guides favorite name for Rick) knows the power of language and at times he is even able to hear some of our thoughts."

Rick felt somewhat relieved. "Will we really be able to publish this book?"

"Do not fear the task of publishing this book. There are many who await these tales and many more tales that await your diligence and commitment. This will be only the first of many books. Still, the project demands your total belief and complete faith. Do not let your doubts and fears delay your chosen destiny."

Rick was so uplifted by these remarks that I began to feel myself riding the waves of his happiness. I must say that, if at times I take this kind of spirit communication for granted, Rick's reactions of delight and unbridled enthusiasm always help me to maintain perspective.

This conversation with our spirit guides was very strong and clear. Although their words came through my vocal chords, I could hear and comprehend everything that was being said. I remember feeling, even while this communication was taking place, that this interaction with my spirit guides was getting more powerful, as though the quality of the connection was improving.

They closed the conversation with the following statement. "Your personal guide, Gwen, is busy working behind the scenes helping us all to converse more easily and clearly. We will have many more conversations like this one in the future and many more letters that address the topic of these wonderful stories and poems and our work together."

For Rick, this midnight rendezvous with our guides became a kind of turning point in his approach to writing. His energy increased, and his dedication solidified. I could tell that Rick was developing a more powerful feeling about his writing and ultimately himself. He no longer behaved as though he had been thrown by chance into his position of storyteller. Rick wrote as though he belonged in that position. During the day, he wrote at lunch time and in between sessions with clients, and at night, he often sat up late at the typewriter; his sounds sometimes lulled me to sleep.

It was on one of those evenings, one during which I had drifted off to sleep listening to the tap tap tap of Rick's two fingered typing, that I awoke suddenly, nearly gasped for my first breath, as though I had run from the tunnel back to my room, the strains of medieval music still ringing in my mind. I grabbed for the notebook on my night table. Rick looked over from his desk and smiled a smile of knowing.

While Rick worked, weaving together the material of this first book, I began a new and awesome adventure into the heart of time, to places yet undiscovered, to worlds beyond my dreams, breathlessly watching and recording the sparkling moments of my wondrous quest.

ABOUT THE AUTHORS

Rick and Louisa Clerici are therapists who live in the Boston area. They operate Clear Mind Systems, a private practice in hypnotherapy. They teach workshops in spiritual development, energy healing, healing with gemstones, mediumship and time travel. They have both made lifetime commitments to the study of metaphysics, consciousness and healing.

Louisa has been a medium since childhood. She has studied with some of the world's leading mediums. Her list of clients includes international entertainment, political and business personalities. Louisa has had a long involvement with the Spiritualist religion, lecturing and demonstrating mediumship at Spiritualist services. Louisa also enjoys performing poetry in "slam" competitions.

Rick has been a singer/songwriter/guitarist since childhood. He has played folk, rock and jazz and has been featured on two recordings. He currently performs and composes with Jamii, the former violinist with Windham Hill's, Shadowfax. They are exploring the healing and transformative qualities of music.

Rick and Louisa are available for lectures, workshops, readings and performances. For more information, or to be on their mailing list, write to:

Rick and Louisa Clerici
P.O. Box 376
Holbrook, MA 02343